# Memoirs
### of
# Elohim and I

CRISTY L. CASTLEBERRY

ISBN 978-1-64349-222-3 (paperback)
ISBN 978-1-64349-275-9 (hardcover)
ISBN 978-1-64349-223-0 (digital)

Christian Faith Publishing, Inc.
832 Park Avenue
Meadville, PA 16335
www.christianfaithpublishing.com

Printed in the United States of America

# Dedication

This book is dedicated to my sweet, fun loving daughter Latiara who has brought me so much joy and reminds me daily of the Godly inheritance I am leaving behind for her and generations to come.

# *Introduction*

This book is written with a heart perfectly positioned toward my Father. This is my love offering to you, my Lord and Savior. It is with a submissive heart that I say thank you.

This book is filled with scripture, encounters, prayers, and revelations God has given to me along my way. He has given me love and strength for people whom I would never have known nor experienced had I not encountered Him along my broken road. He makes *all* broken things beautiful in time, and it is with my heart poured out that I sit at His feet and will never retreat to that brokenness. I pray that anyone reading this book not only feels hope but has a miraculous encounter with the One who loves you most and the One who loves you best. Be encouraged, be intentional, and be blessed.

# 1

Don't be scared to dream big because if your idea is bigger than you are and you can't do it in your strength, then you know it's God's dream for you.

Many years ago, the Lord gave me this vision to write this book to encourage and lift His amazing people through prayers, encounters, testimonies, thoughts, and revelations He has given to me. I made every excuse I could just like Moses over the past four years. I don't have an editor, so what does God do? He sends me an editor. I could go on with all the crazy and—well, let's just face it—rather lame excuses. He told me He needs to reach His people through this book, and to be honest, that terrified me!

As I sat down to write, I asked Holy Spirit to be my guide, give me a name, and more than that, give me His book. So as my fingers flew, I felt the presence of the Lord like never before. Hunger like never before, like this, is what I had been made for. I was called for such as time as this.

I pray this encourages you and others to pursue godly dreams and to trust in God with *all* your heart, and not lean on your own understanding but in *all* your ways acknowledge and submit to Him and He will direct your path. (Prov.5 3:5–6, ESV)

Be intentional. Be blessed.

# 2

Sometimes, you just need a respectable kick in your pants—spiritual pants, that is.

I am so thankful for a godly friend who did just that this evening! I needed God to send someone else so that I could understand what He was trying to tell me, only I didn't know I needed that. I needed to get out of my way. In particular, what I needed was to fast. I wasn't getting a clear picture of it even though it was right beside me. I spent all day not eating, praying, being a mess, and crying out to God for the answer on what I was supposed to fast on. My spirit was not at rest with me picking food. I just assumed that it would be food because that was what He had me do before and similar times throughout the year. Well, I was wrong, and the moment I got what it was, I started to cry. That realization of what God was trying to tell me all along put my spirit at ease in a moment's time, and rest and peace came over me. Moral of the story, it doesn't always have to be food that God leads you to fast. It can be other things.

"While they were worshiping the Lord and fasting, the Holy Spirit said, 'Set apart for me Barnabas and Saul for the work to which I have called them'" (Acts 13:2, NIV). Much like me right now, He has set me apart for the work to which He has called me. I was supposed to have this book finished in 2016, and now it is 2017. I am genuinely excited for His masterpiece to be released this coming year. Yes, I am standing in and claiming His promises. It is done in Jesus's mighty name!

Be intentional. Be blessed.

# 3

Have you ever broken a mirror and it shattered into a dozen pieces? What kind of mirror are you reflecting? Broken or whole?

Are you a broken mirror reflecting your pain, bitterness, or maybe reflecting the labels that someone has given to you like, ugly, stupid, fat, forgetful; I could go on. These things just seem to wreck you at your core, and no matter how many times you try not to believe them, your heart somehow accepts them. Our identity is stolen from us, and we think this is just the way we are, that this is all we will ever be. I am what you say I am.

I used to have this same broken mirror I mentioned above until I went to a Christian counselor, and God's truth about who I am was spoken to my heart. It took a good long year starting back from when I was a child, working through those painful memories, feelings, false identifications, and labels. At one point, I couldn't even cry. I was emotionless. I would try to be vulnerable; it would come out angry. I had to learn to trust again and that it was safe to share my feelings. I learned to accept the truth of God's word about myself and began to heal.

I am a child of God. I am fearfully and wonderfully made. I could go on and on now, but the truth is, I couldn't back then until God restored my identity. I say all of this to explain to you if you are walking through this that you have a purpose, plan, and a future that God can restore. I no longer reflect the broken mirror that previous generations have passed down to me. That broken mirror stopped with me. My child knows who she is and whose she is, and I reflect a full-length unbroken mirror back to her instead of the broken one that was reflected to me so many times as a child. I had a horrific childhood, but as an adult, I get to make choices. And it's never too late to partake in a happy adulthood. Jesus can restore whatever it is that was taken from you.

Try this: Go to the bathroom and stare at your reflection. What do you think about yourself? What do you say about yourself? Take inventory. Doing this will reveal to you quite a bit about yourself. You can do this with children as well. Periodically, I do this with my daughter. Is your mirror reflecting God's truth or the lies of Satan? If there is a crack in your mirror, find someone whom you can talk to about it who is a full-length uncracked mirror and can reflect God's love to you and help you begin to heal. It is God's will that our lives are healed.

Be intentional. Be blessed.

# 4

Do you rejoice when others do well?

You know if you are not, then it is a direct reflection of what's hidden in your heart. Why aren't you rejoicing for your brother or sister in Christ? Do they have something you desire so badly? Reality check: if God can do it for them, He can do it for you! Check your motives, intentions, etc., and start with yourself and your heart.

James 4:3 (NIV) says, "When you ask, you do not receive, because you ask with wrong motives, that you may spend what you get on your pleasures."

Enough said.

Be intentional. Be blessed.

# 5

One thing I have asked God for is to be able to see people and love people the way He does with my spiritual eyes and my spiritual heart. Luke 11:9 (NIV) says, "So I say to you: Ask, and it will be given to you; seek, and you will find; knock, and the door will be opened to you."

The Lord has entrusted me this precious gift. When I pray for someone, He will drop in my spirit what they are walking through such as loneliness, depression, heartbreak, you name it. He allows me to speak life and wholeness using His word, giving them a hope and a future in Him.

Take notice that I say He has entrusted me, He allows me, a hope, and a future in Him, not in Cristy Castleberry but in Jesus Christ our Lord and Savior. He is our only Savior and only Hope. "The Lord is close to the brokenhearted and saves those who are crushed in spirit" (Ps. 34:18, NIV).

What are you asking God for today? Are they good things or godly things?

Be intentional. Be blessed.

# 6

As I embark on this eight-day spiritual fasting journey with my brothers and sisters in Christ, I will be fasting solid food and only be doing juices. I have a spiritual craving like never before. I entered this fast with a high expectation of hearing from the Lord. As it says in the Bible, certain things can be overcome only by prayer and fasting. "Children, you are from God and have overcome them, for He who is in you is greater than he who is in the world" (1 John 4:4, ESV).

I pray for a spiritual strengthening, a boldness and equipping to spread the Gospel like never before, an awakening for our nation from its sleepy slumber, for our nation to repent and turn from its wicked ways, a hedge of protection and covering for our spiritual leaders and their families as they continue to lead us and guide us during these dark days ahead of us, that righteousness will prevail, and the truth be made known to everyone so that generations would rise and be the change they want to see based on biblical truths and knowledge. I also pray that the Word of God would be read all over the world and would penetrate the hearts and lives of all men and women.

In Jesus's name, I pray. Amen.

Be intentional. Be blessed.

# 7

I hear those chains falling....
Break every chain, break every chain.

—Tasha Cobbs, "Break Every Chain"

I'm so thankful for divine appointments. One evening, on our way home from Tennessee to Alabama, we stopped at a gas station, and when I stepped out of the vehicle, one of the gas station attendants was outside. I knew right away that I was on assignment as the Lord prompted. I wasn't exactly sure until I was in the gas station for a little while, and talking to her revealed to me what exactly He needed me to do. Her mom had recently been hospitalized due to pneumonia. He needed me to speak life and hope to her about this situation. She needed to hear that I will pray for her mom and know sincerely there would be a follow-up action behind it and that someone loves and cares for her. I'm sincerely praying for her mom Donna.

When I was in Next Steps 301 and did the survey for spiritual gifting areas, I scored high in Missions, Prayer, and something else. And I told God, "Missions, okay. Prayer, that's not for me. That's for Pastor Steve." Pastor Steve is a wonderful man of God and has the wonderful gift of prayer. And I quickly moved on. Needless to say, God has placed me in every opportunity since then to pray for and to do His will. Now I humbly submit to His spiritual gifting for me and said, "Okay, Lord, I get it. I'll do it." I was missing the blessing. In fact, I was blocking my blessing. Since then, I have stepped out in obedience and prayed for all sorts of ailments, anointed areas of the body that needed healing, and witnessed the miracles of the power of Jesus Christ in ways I never thought possible. And I can tell you this: there is no greater honor in this lifetime than to do the work for His kingdom. When someone messages me, calls me, and asks for prayer, I take it very seriously. I always want to point them back to the one and only Savior, not to me. Apart from Him, we are nothing and can do nothing, but in Him, we can do all things.

Your faith can move mountains. Have you moved any lately? All power and authority have been given to us. It has been declared in the Bible, His living word. Are you walking in, proclaiming in His power and authority? If you don't believe, declare, and claim His promises, how will you be able to reach this broken world? We walk not as victims but as victors! Rise! We are soldiers for Christ. Put on your spiritual armor and be ready to sacrifice.

Be intentional. Be blessed.

## 8

I want to see Your face,
I want to know Your heart,
I want to walk with You
Every day of my life God

—House of Fires, "See Your Face"

I love Mondays! I love warming my car up early for my child so she doesn't have to freeze to death when she gets in! (It was 18 degrees this morning.) God gave me her, a gift and a blessing whom I get to wake up to. I thank God for getting to pray with her on any occasion; but the way to school seems to be our special times because we could pray and, when time permits, read a devotional right before she gets out of the car to go to school. I just love the sweet spirit she has about her. Reflections of her sweet spirit are seen when she smiles as she turns to get out of the car, and Latiara blinks her eyes to let me know she loves me. We have our unique sign so that no matter where she is, whether it's across the room or right beside me, we can communicate love to one another. These special times remind me of how great our Heavenly Father's love is for us and how He reflects a love back to us like no other.

Be intentional. Be blessed.

# 9

As I came out of the church and couldn't find my car for the billionth time last night, we were—I hate to admit it—roaming the parking lot and it occurred to me that all who wander are not lost and all who are lost aren't necessarily wandering around.

In Luke 15, the parable of the lost sheep is told to us by Jesus.

> Then Jesus told them this parable: "Suppose one of you has a hundred sheep and loses one of them. Doesn't he leave the ninety-nine in the open country and go after the lost sheep until he finds it? And when he finds it, he joyfully puts it on his shoulders and goes home. Then he calls his friends and neighbors together and says, 'Rejoice with me; I have found my lost sheep.' I tell you that in the same way there will be more rejoicing in heaven over one sinner who repents than over ninety-nine righteous persons who do not need to repent." (Luke 15: 3–7, NIV)

Most of the time, we are this lost sheep waiting for someone to find us to bring us home. When sin blinds us, we are wandering around in the dark trying to find our way when we can't see clearly. Much like me searching for my car so that I could go home. Until Jesus encounters us, we will always be searching, wandering, trying to find our way around in the dark. I could have freaked out and hit the panic button and chosen to alert everyone in the parking lot of my distress, or I could hit the actual peace button that I know works every time. I selected the Prince of Peace button—Jesus! I prayed, "Father help me to find my way even when it's dark. When I am wandering, and have no clue where You are sending me, even when I am not lost help me to discover my way, help me find my car so that I can return home just like the returning of the one ewe. I love you, Father, and I know you are a good Father and you love me. And as your child, I wait for you expectant that you will answer me and help me find my way. In Jesus's mighty name. Amen."

Then guess what happened? Moments later, my car was found, not without Jesus's help, not all by myself. He cares about the little things; He desires for us to seek Him. How many of us wait on Him expectant? Are you a lost sheep? If so, it's never too late. If He does it for me, He will do it for you. Even in the little stuff, God sees; He is Father God El Roi.

Be intentional. Be blessed.

# 10

Why are you cast down, O my inner self? And why should you moan over me and be disquieted within me? Hope in God and wait expectantly for Him, for I shall yet praise Him, my help my God. —Psalm 42:5, AMPC

Discouragement demolishes hope. Failure quickly leads to more failure. And once we allow our minds to be set and say, "This is the way it will always be," Satan has won that battle over us. All hope gets lost, but if we change our thoughts, we can alter the outcome of our lives. We may be knocked down, but we don't have to stay there. We can get back up again and move boldly and confidently in Christ Jesus, our Lord and Savior. We are a new creation in Him. What Satan meant for harm, He can use it for good.

Be intentional. Be blessed.

# 11

And I will do whatever you ask in my name, so
that the Father may be glorified in the Son.

—John 14:13, NIV

Today and most days, I am reflecting on the awe of God! His faithfulness and timing always blow me away. He is Father God El Roi;
He is the God who sees. It's crazy amazing how obedience to Him
leads to Him pouring out a blessing. I don't even have room enough
to receive in my own heart.

Thank you for allowing me to come pray with you and stand
in agreement with you, Shelly. So this leads to a super awesome testimony. I was/is/am Shelly's life group coleader. I was supposed to take
her some sheets for our life group. Shelly had been very sick having
wiped out her eardrum. The wiping out of her eardrum had been
confirmed by two doctors from urgent care. She was supposed to go
to an ENT specialist the next day to get checked out and see what
they could do for her, if anything.

Going back to me. So the Lord spoke very clearly to me and
told me to go, but I have this terrible habit of arguing with Elohim,
then doing what He tells me to. So I said I didn't need to go because
she could just print off the papers. Then He put it to me plainly:
"Just Go!" Little did I know it was a divine appointment, and so He
had me pray for her and anoint her ear. The next day, she goes to the
ENT specialist, and the doctor put in a scope to look in her ear. Oh
my gosh here it goes: they said, "I don't know how but your eardrum
is there." We knew how! God is so good! Won't He do it!

Be intentional. Be blessed.

# 12

So the other day, I was very sick and had to seek urgent care. Feeling terrible, I thought it was streptococcus because Latiara had it last week. Lo and behold, they are treating me for flu. I'm not sure where I got it, but rest assured they had me on medicine and away from peeps. I was somber because I wasn't able to serve in Celebration Place and share the love of Jesus Christ to the little ones with Joyce, my other awesome sister in Christ whom I served under, even though I had already prepared for it.

I felt like I was letting Joyce down, and since Latiara was to be at her Valentine's event at church as well, I was beginning to feel like I let her down too. My awesome sister in Christ Angelique came and got Latiara from urgent care and took her to the event. Talk about being the hands and feet of Jesus. Also, Joyce was so excellent too and kind to me when I told her I wouldn't be able to serve. Again, the hands and feet of Jesus by her kindness and compassion.

As I sat back in the room of the urgent care clinic, I realized this was a divine appointment or setup, not the sickness but for me to share the love of Jesus Christ with the young nurse going through my history. She was asking me about the history of my parents, and I got to share what God has done for our mom through prayer and anointing. Then, about my other amazing sister in Christ, Shelly. The young girl looked at me and said, "Wow, this was meant for me today. I needed to hear this."

For me, it was definitely a divine appointment. You never know what incredible opportunities He is going to give you to witness. Even through sickness, I have learned to be obedient to the Holy Spirit. He can turn a setback into a setup so you can look up.

Be intentional. Be blessed.

# 13

Father God, help us.

We must be ever mindful of the words we come to speak and ask ourselves, "Will they build up?" For words can cut us to the depths of our core. If only we could grasp this, we would speak only words of hope that bring blessings, encouragement, and help one another to grow.

I pray this in Your precious name. Amen

Be intentional. Be blessed.

# 14

Scripture challenge:

> And therefore, the Lord [earnestly] waits [expecting, looking, and longing] to be gracious to you; and therefore He lifts Himself up, that He may have mercy on you and show loving-kindness to you. For the Lord is a God of justice. Blessed (happy, fortunate, to be envied) are all those who [earnestly] wait for Him, who expect and look, and long for Him [for His victory]. (Isa. 30:18, AMPC)

God's timing is not our timing. What should waiting for Him look like?

We should wait with an expectancy. Many times will we ask Him for something then turn around and cancel it due to our doubt and unbelief by saying such things as, "Well, I asked Him, but I don't think it will happen." Or "It's not happening in my timing, so it's just not so."

We should wait with the Word (the *Bible*). We should, while waiting, be feeding our spiritual being with what God says. Claim and declare His promises. Satan loves to get in where he doesn't fit in by twisting things just about when we are ready to receive our blessing. He will remind us of how much we don't deserve it, how unworthy we truly are. And then *bam!* He's got us. God points to our relationship where Satan points to our shortcomings; that's the difference.

While waiting patiently, practice putting on the full armor of God and then put it into action. I literally will complete the physical actions before the mirror while verbally putting it on. Once suited up daily, pray a prayer for God to use you as His soldier. While you faithfully wait on God's blessings, pray that He would use you to be a blessing to someone else. A lot of times, our blessings are received not by the way we think we ought to receive them but by the way God intervenes and uses someone else to bless us.

I have had to wait years. Yes, it was tough, and yes, it was very painful at times before I have received an answer. When you wait, well, it's a difficult journey but not an impossible one, and God will bless those who are faithful.

Be intentional. Be blessed.

# 15

By this, all will know that you are my disciples if
you have love for one another.

—John 13:35, WEB

We are all more competent witnesses when we become the canvas
on which God displays and writes His beauty or handsomeness to
be known.

What are you doing as a disciple of Christ to show love for
another?

Be encouraged. Be intentional. Be blessed.

# 16

If it is possible, as much as depends on you, live peaceably with all men.

—Romans 12:18, NKJV

We must be diplomats even if others refuse to be. One day, we will stand to give an account of our life before God. All the "but he/she made me do it," all the excuses and justifications will not change that we are accountable and responsible before God for what we say, do, and live out. Every day, we have choices that we are faced with. Some are incredible, some not so much.

In this tireless world, we want an easy solution, a quick fix when troubles come our way. But in this broken world, it's not always the way things work out. You will be tested daily, interacting with life, people, your best friends, enemies, etc. How you respond in contrast to your reaction to them can be the difference between a blessing and a curse. Am I saying it's easy? No. Am I saying that you will be perfect? No. But what I am saying is obedience is our job; the rest we leave to God. Situations and people can be tough, but we must prayerfully rely on God's grace and wisdom to deal with them from day to day.

Try this, the next time you're faced with a desperate situation, ask God to see the eternal. Ask to see or perceive what that person is saying or doing. Satan likes to get us distracted in these moments with what the person is saying or doing so he can sucker punch us and get us off-balance and away from God. But take heart, guard your gates, and fix your eyes on God, and He will reveal to you what is going on in a situation. Give Satan God's Word to choke on. While he is choking, you rebuke him and proclaim in the name of Jesus who you are; what you stand for; and that he has no place in your relationships, family, marriage, house, etc. Because as for you and your house, you will serve the Lord.

Can I get an amen?

Be intentional. Be blessed.

# 17

Our meekness will be put to trial before we are put in places of authority because God wants to verify we will lead through His direction rather than our ambitions.

Romans 12:16 (NIV) tells us not to be wise in our estimation. We must be cautious not to influence those around us through our power and might. We must humbly submit to the authority of God.

We are called to seek and save that which is lost, and we must do so humbly, not in a tranquil or undignified manner but in the bold and graceful humility that God intended for us to walk in.

Be intentional. Be blessed.

# 18

Then I acknowledged my sin to You, and did not cover up my iniquity.… And You forgave the guilt of my sin.

—Psalm 32:5, NIV

Being discovered is relieving. In Psalm 32:3–4 (NIV), David wrote of this: "When I kept silent, my bones wasted away through my groaning all day long. Day and night Your hand was heavy on me."

Why do we postpone so long to deal with personal failures that weigh us down so worryingly in our intellect? When we cover up what is well known, what do we stand to gain? After all, we have already been "discovered" by the Lord, so there is no need to pretend any longer. Recognizing this, confession then brings about relief and starts the process of healing and restoration that God wants to do in our lives.

Sin brings fear; confession brings freedom.

Be intentional. Be blessed.

# 19

Father God, I lift Lisa's daughter-in-law up to you and her precious little one that is inside of her named Lannan in Jesus's mighty name! You know the distress that this child and his mother are under. Father God, we come into agreement right now in the name of Jesus that Lisa's daughter-in-law and Lannan are healed in Jesus's mighty name. Father God, we pray for the cancellation of any assignment of the enemy on their lives and their family.

You say by Your stripes they are healed, Lord God, and we boldly proclaim that they are healed in Your precious Son's name—Jesus! We pray for a hedge of protection around them, Lord, as they go out and come back. Lord, we pray for your answers. We know that no weapon formed that will try to come in opposition to them shall ever prosper! We pray for the release of trauma that the issue has caused within every cell of their bodies; and we claim and declare healing and wholeness to their precious bodies, minds, and spirits, Lord God. We plead for the blood of Jesus over them and ask you to reconcile every issue in Jesus's name. We know that you are a loving God and You said ask and it shall be given, so we ask and stand in agreement together with your word, Lord God. And it is by faith that they believe and receive this blessing of healing in wholeness in Jesus's name. Amen.

\*\*\*

This precious child's life was spared, and God answered this prayer.

Be intentional. Be blessed.

# 20

Trust in The Lord, and do good. Rest in The
Lord, and wait patiently for Him.

—Psalm 37:3, KJV

Patience should characterize the life of every believer who is trying to
be a disciple of Christ.

Do you have a game plan with God? If so, do you believe in
it? If we believe in it, we will wear Satan down and get to him. If we
break away from God's style and play Satan's style, we are in trouble.
And if we let the emotions of the flesh command the game instead of
reason, we will not function effectively. I caution you to play God's
game. Eventually, if you stick to God's style, the honorable class will
tell the end. This does not mean we will always outscore our oppo-
nent, but it does ensure we will not beat ourselves.

In Psalm 37, God is saying, "In conclusion, do what's proper.
And trust Me, regardless of how poorly you may seem to be losing,
just do My will and leave the result to Me. I'll make sure that eventually you'll be a winner." You can't lose if you stay with God's game
plan.

"We are more than conquerors" (Rom. 8:37).

Even if I seem to be walking through the valley of the shadow
of death, my eyes are secured on you Lord; I will not move, I will not
be shaken, You are with me.

Be intentional. Be blessed.

# 21

Father God, I lift Angelique up to you in Jesus's mighty name! Father God, we come into agreement right now in the name of Jesus that Angelique is healed in Jesus's mighty name. Father God, we pray for the cancellation of any assignment of the enemy on her life and her family.

You say by Your stripes she is healed, Lord God, and we boldly proclaim that she is healed in Your precious Son's name—Jesus! We pray for a hedge of protection around her, Lord, and her family as she goes out and comes back.

Lord, we pray for Your answers. We know that no weapon formed against her shall ever flourish! We pray for the release of trauma that the fever is causing within every cell of her body and claim and declare healing and wholeness in her precious body, mind, and spirit, Lord God. We plead the blood of Jesus over her and ask you to reconcile every issue in Jesus's name. We know that you are a loving God, and You said, "Ask, and it shall be given." So we ask and stand in agreement together with your word, Lord God, and it is by faith that we bear witness and believe this blessing on her behalf interceding with you, Lord, and she receives this blessing of healing and wholeness in Jesus's mighty name! Amen.

The Lord healed her.

Be intentional. Be blessed.

# 22

Discovering bravery is to position ourselves when we genuflect before the Lord.

"'Be strong, all you people of the land,' says The Lord, 'and work; for I am with you'" (Hag. 2:4, NIV)

Be intentional. Be blessed.

# 23

How sweet are Your words to my taste, sweeter
than honey to my mouth!

Psalm 119:103, NIV

Most of us live in a realm where food is abundant and people are
well fed. That's why most of us have no evidence of the symptoms
of starvation. On the inside, victims have a longing for nourishment
for the body. As time passes without food or nourishment, our body
weakens, the mind dulls, and the desire for something to eat dimin-
ishes. Starving people reach a point when they don't even want food
that is set before them.

Now let's talk about spiritual starvation. It follows pretty much
the same course. If we have been feeding every day on God's word,
it's okay to feel famished when we neglect our quiet time. But if we
continue, we may lose all desire to study His Word. In fact, we may
be starving ourselves.

How much time do we spend on reading the Bible and ponder-
ing on its truths? Do we miss the Word when we neglect it? Thomas
Guthrie once wrote, "If you find yourself loving any pleasure better
than your prayers, any book better than your Bible, any persons better than Christ, or any indulgence better than the hope of heaven
take alarm."

If you have lost your taste for the "Bread of Life," it's time to
confess and ask God to revive it. Avoid spiritual starvation!

A well-read Bible is an indication of a well-nourished soul.

Be intentional. Be blessed.

# 24

Responsibility is our response to God's ability. If we are going to be accountable, we must respond to the prospects that God places in front of us.

Heavenly Father, please pardon me for not always being responsive to You and Your ability. Help me to emphasize not on circumstances and hindrances but on Your love and abundant resources. I ask this through the name of your completely obedient Son. Amen.

Be intentional. Be blessed.

# 25

To forget the former things, we will have to leave our past where it belongs at the cross.

Be intentional. Be blessed.

# 26

Remember, the life we live here won't last long, but the legacy we leave will last forever and the way we face and fight our battles in this life will determine our legacy.

God bless you.

Be intentional. Be blessed.

## 27

Wow, I am listening to Father God. I was woken up from my slumber at three in the morning and led to pray. After praying, I was led to get my Bible and read. I closed my eyes and asked Father God what He would have me read.

"Ecclesiastes."

"Um… okay. Where?"

"I will guide you." The message is found in chapter 12:1–14. It's about seeking God early in life, remembering our Creator, and what the whole duty of man is.

> Fear God and keep His commandments,
> For this is man's all.
> For God, will bring every work into judgment,
> Including every secret thing, whether
> good or evil. (Eccles. 12:1–4, NHEB)

I am thankful for my Heavenly Father's guidance. I am thankful that as we listen and seek Him, He gives us a clear understanding of our lives, people in our lives, and what plans He has for us to glorify Him.

Be intentional. Be blessed.

## 28

For Christ's love compels us.

"Let your focus be on love so, that you will naturally reflect the fruit of the spirit" (2 Cor. 5:14, NIV)

"But the fruit of the Spirit is love, joy, peace, forbearance, kindness, goodness, faithfulness, gentleness, and self-control. Against such things, there is no law" (Gal. 5:22–23, NIV).

Rather than trying to conjure up the correct attitudes and behavior, let love be your default position. Then you will be willing to enter into any circumstance graciously and have no regrets.

Be intentional. Be blessed.

# 29

We laugh, we cry
Sometimes we're broken, and
we don't know why,
I'm tired, and I lose my way,
You help me find faith, OOO
You give me hope, in spite of everything,
You show me, love, even with so much pain
So I'll take this life and live like
I was given another try
Just give me another try.

(Between the Trees)

Be intentional. Be blessed.

# 30

"Just as you trusted Christ to save you, trust Him, too, for each day's problems. Live in vital union with Him" (Col. 2:6–7, TLB).

Be intentional. Be blessed.

# 31

Had an awesome day! Working out felt great!

Zumba, Zumba, Zumba. It's been six months since the 105.5-degree fever that nearly crippled me. I prayed about my sickness and felt led to completely get off the seven different medications they prescribed me and just take a vitamin pack and an iron pill. And guess what? I felt great. I can now do the minor tasks, like laundry, without the pain in every one of my joints. Thank you to all who have prayed for me, called me, sent cards and flowers, and supported me. I thank God for each one of you. God is so good!

In my future book about my life, I will go into further details about this battle and what I was thinking, feeling, and the account of my daughter and how she felt at the age of seven.

Be intentional. Be blessed.

# 32

Have I not commanded you? Be strong and courageous. Do not be afraid; do not be discouraged, for the Lord your God will be with you wherever you go.

—Joshua 1:9, NIV

Be strong and do not be discouraged; I am your Father and I go before you.

What would we do if we really knew the power that dwells inside of us? Are you a world changer by the power of Jesus Christ? The He who is inside of you (1 John 4:4, KJV).

We know, but do we really know as we ought to?

Life is not about what I can get out of it but what I can give back. Because I have been given to abundantly, I can freely give to others. There were points in my life when I had nothing, including not having a place to stay. Yes, that means being homeless.

I didn't begin where I am today. I came from an impoverished, broken background, but He redeems. He turns what the evil one meant for bad into something beautiful and amazing. God ordered years of my steps and is still ordering every step that I take.

I still sit in awe, I look around and get choked up because He loves the least of us; He loves me. He saw me then, and I can guarantee He sees *you* now. He gives us hope and a future. Because of this, I am not afraid or ashamed to speak out about my life and what I have been through. My test is my testimony, and God uses it to reach others for His glorious kingdom.

Be intentional. Be blessed.

# 33

So sweet, someone messaged me and said they passed a field full of daffodils and it reminded them of me. Nice to know I left a real lasting impact on someone else's life.

We need to think about the impact and the legacy we are leaving.

Ask yourself: What legacy am I leaving the world with?

Be intentional. Be blessed.

# 34

"Do not merely look out for your own personal interests, but also for the interest of others" (Phil. 2:4, NASB).

Be intentional. Be blessed.

# 35

I went to the doctor last week and had my blood drawn and went back to get the results. My results reveal that I am severely deficient in vitamin D. Well, I would rather be vitamin D deficient any day than vitamin C deficient because you see, in the kingdom, I should always be severely vitamin D deficient, meaning lack of *D* for devil, and abounding in vitamin C. That is vitamin Christ!

If we took vitamin Christ like we take vitamin C to boost our immune system and to keep us feeling great, well, imagine what it could lead to: *restoration*, better attitude, healthier emotional life, as well as physical and spiritual lives. Families being made whole again, marriages restored, you name it. The impact for God's kingdom would be so great!

If you take vitamin Christ daily in the body, it acts as an antioxidant; you will notice that you start to feel better and better. A substance such as vitamin C removes damaging oxidizing agents (or sins and bondages) in a living being.

Taking vitamin Christ will help to protect your mind, body, and spirit from the damage caused by Satan's attempts; thus, keeping the fiery darts from penetrating our souls. It's also known that ascorbic acid is meant to be absorbed in our body. Just like the Word, it's expected to be consumed. So take the time to make sure you are getting the right vitamin C.

Be intentional. Be blessed.

# 36

Are you packing?

"To the Jews who had believed him, Jesus said, 'If you hold to my teaching you are really my disciples. Then you will know the truth, and the truth will set you free" (John 8:31–32, NIV).

I am recently reminded of an encounter with one of my good friends. My friend and I were in a beauty supply store on Hwy 72. She had purchased some items, and we were getting ready to head out the door. We set off the security alarm. The lady at the store then said, "Oh, you packing a gun?"

My friend said, "No, I'm packing the other *G* (God)." We laughed about it at the time, but how true is it that we are to arm ourselves with God? The truth is the Word; and we can combat any attack, lie, stronghold, etc. with His godly weapons that He equips us with. It's absolute truth. We have the ability because He dwells inside us. So we can put on the full armor of God and go out boldly and confidently.

Be intentional. Be blessed.

# 37

The higher the calling the greater the intensity of the attacks become.

As we were on our way to Sharing Your Faith Life-group this morning, we went under a sign on 565-E, and something dropped and it shattered the sunroof of my car. I had already known something was going to happen because of the amount of resistance that had occurred this morning before we left our house.

I am so thankful that God prepares us to respond instead of react. I just pulled the car over ever so calmly, and we got out and looked at it then got back in the car. I called my insurance company. I am so thankful in times like this one that I didn't react; I responded. If I had reacted, I could have overcompensated and swerved into someone else's lane, causing unnecessary harm. I am so thankful for the Holy Spirit, the quiet calm in a raging storm who helps me to stay in my lane and keep my eyes fixed on Jesus, even when things in the external are bad or look bad.

Romans 8:28 (NIV) said, "And we know that in all things God works for the good of those who love him, who have been called according to his purpose."

My daughter asked, "Are we still going to outreach?"

I replied, "Yes, yes we are."

"But in that coming day, no weapon turned against you will succeed. You will silence every voice raised up to accuse you. These benefits are enjoyed by the servants of the Lord; their vindication will come from me. I, the Lord, have spoken!" (Isa. 54:17, NLT).

It was an excellent day in outreach and we saw from previous weeks the fruit of the God seeds that were planted, and prayers were answered. I am honored to get to serve and do life with these wonderful brothers and sisters in Christ.

If He is for us, who can be against us?

Be intentional. Be blessed.

# 38

So as I was staring at my ripped jeans, Jesus reminded me that's how I came to him back then: dirty, torn, and tattered. Now my ripped jeans, are clean, and a patch behind the rips serve as my reminder that Jesus still heals, and He healed me in the depths of my brokenness right where I was at. Looking closer at my ripped jeans, a pattern of strings overlay that patch much like stripes, reminding me.

"But he was wounded for our transgressions, he was bruised for our iniquities: the chastisement of our peace was upon him; and with his stripes, we are healed" (Isa. 53:5, KJV).

He makes all broken things beautiful in His time if we only allow Him to transform us from the inside out.

Just a thought: I could have easily looked at my ripped jeans and said, "Look at my life. From the womb, the doctor's begged my mother to abort me because she had cancer. By the age of one and a half, my dad attempted to murder my mom. Being sexually abused at a young age over and over, then being shipped from foster home to foster home, I could have used this as an excuse to remain a victim saying, 'This is the way I will always be, nobody wants me, abandoned, abused, unloved, rejected.' But instead, I see when I look at my ripped jeans a victor, not the victim; conqueror, not conquered; wanted, not wounded; redeemed, not rejected; healed, not harmed; and loved so much so that He thinks I am to die for and He did just that!"

God doesn't just see where we are at, but He looks to our future to what we are to become. And if He can do it for me, He too can set you free!

Be encouraged. Be intentional. Be blessed.

# 39

Have you had your vision checked? Are you overdue for your eye exam? Some of us haven't had our eyes checked in years—our spiritual vision.

If we don't get our spiritual eyes checked often, we don't realize how far off we tend to drift away from the Lord. Our vision gets blurred or fuzzy; you may even see spots and begin to wonder if your vision is going bad or you're just seeing things and dismiss it as simply nothing.

It all starts with what we let in or what we are viewing with our eye gate often. An eye gate is one of the gates to our soul, and the soul can be moved by what one allows to enter. Something that you see can cause emotion. These are based on the 5 senses being the 5 gates. See Matthew 6:22.

Now what do you do if you need your vision checked? Well, you would call up the eye doctor and make an appointment to get rechecked or evaluated. They would give you an extensive exam and ask you if you see clearer with one or two, three or four, etc., until they can come to a determination that your eyesight has changed and you need an adjustment and then they write you a new prescription.

So what does that mean in spiritual terms?

If you need your spiritual vision checked, you need to make that call—call on the Lord and make an appointment for Him to meet you right where you are at. Pray to have eyes to see clearly, ears to hear His wisdom as He speaks to you, and a heart to receive and obey His word. He is not going to ask you if you can see clearer with one or two, three or four because He is the number one and you will always see clearer choosing number one, not two, three or four.

When God reveals to you that your eyesight has changed, meaning you have drifted away from the Lord, He will then write your prescription. True godly repentance, daily dose of prayer, and spending time in God's word, read a daily devotional, going to church, followed up by accountability. Join a Bible study or life group, connect, after all we are personally responsible for our own relationship with Him. What we feed lives and what we starve dies. Die to your flesh daily then follow all this up by taking your eyes off of self and serve someone else, whether it is in outreach in your community, at church, or even in another city or town. And before you know it, your spiritual vision will improve significantly; your vision will be restored. So the cure is Christ and keeping our eyes fixed on Him.

This is the revelation that He gave me the other day as I went to the eye doctor to get contacts. Without new contacts, I couldn't even read the eye exam letters, but as soon as I popped in those contacts, I could read even the tiniest letters. It was unbelievable! That's how amazing God is. Apart from Him, I can see nothing in my view correctly, but with Him, I can see everything!

Praising God daily.

Be intentional. Be blessed.

# 40

So, when you buy a new home, some people will solicit at your door-step asking you to buy their home security system. Most of the time, it's at the most inopportune times like when you are having your stuff delivered or perhaps having a Bible study. You politely decline and tell them you are in the middle of Bible study, and they tell you, "Okay, can I come back in ten minutes?"

Again, a polite "no, thank you." When the next person shows up to sell you a home security system, you politely open the door and listen again as they tell you that you are the only person who doesn't have a sign in your yard for a security system. Then as the Holy Spirit springs up out of you, you let them know you have the best home security system there is. And as they lean in and say, "Really? What is it?" You know at this point they are captivated, and you let them know it's God. You also explain to them you are a combat veteran and you are always packing a *G*, again God; but they are thinking the other *G*, gun, they say thank you for your service as they are slowly backing away and let you know they won't be bothering you again.

They didn't see the sign in the yard, but it was right in front of the door. A sign clearly displaying my home security system. It reads as such: "Christ is the Head of This House!!!" I pondered as they walked away how often we don't even notice our own security system as Christians: God. We see Him in everything, yet some see Him in nothing. If we can see Him in the little things, we will be able to see Him in the big things. We need Him every second and every hour of every day.

"I am the vine; you are the branches. If you remain in me and I in you, you will bear much fruit; apart from me, you can do nothing" (John 15:5, NIV).

Be intentional. Be blessed.

# 41

"Accept one another, then, just as Christ accepted you, in order to bring praise to God." (Rom. 15:7, NIV)

Be intentional. Be blessed.

# 42

In as much as you did it to one of the least of these my brethren, you did it to Me.

—Matthew 25:40, NKJV

Ever been *called out*? When He rings, you better answer the *call*.

As I look around most Sundays, I see hundreds of people at church. I spend a brief minute—okay, okay, for me, a long minute wondering about and waiting expectantly on God's call. How can I make a difference?

How many times in the rush of the ordinary church life do we overlook or pass by our call? Even if we only make a difference to one, it matters. Jesus never let crowds discourage Him from helping individuals. Jesus calls us to do the same. We must recognize the importance of this as mentioned above in the scripture. I know we want to reach everyone, but do what you can to help one at a time and prayerfully leave the rest to God.

Be intentional. Be blessed.

# 43

I am freaking out right now! God just absolutely blew me away again by His awesomeness! He entrusted some parents to come to me about a particular situation, and God used me to contact their child. Of course, I prayed about it and let the Holy Spirit guide me as to what needed to be said. It's never me; it's always God. He just uses me to do His excellent work. What an honor! After I had contacted the child, I did not contact them again. I continued to pray. Five days later, their daughter contacted me. Today, God answered a mother and a father's prayer. During that time, I told them never to stop praying. "God hears your faithful cry out on your child's behalf."

Lord, I am amazed by You!

I humbly thank You, God.

Be intentional. Be blessed.

# 44

Thank you to all of the soldiers who have given their lives, are serving, and have served; it's because of you that I can wake up every morning to my little girl's (who's not so little anymore) smiling face and know that we are safe. I love you all dearly! I am blessed beyond measure to have served with the elite. I will never forget serving in Operation Iraqi Freedom in 2003–2004.

May we remember today and what it's all about. It is a day to celebrate and honor American veterans for their patriotism, love of country, and willingness to serve and sacrifice for family, friends, etc. I say thank you again, and I honor you today and forever. For your selfless service, honor, and integrity, may your sacrifices never go unnoticed. I love you. My brothers, sisters, mothers, and fathers who have served and are still serving. Freedom is never cheap; it's always bought with a price. Thank you for your willingness to pay the ultimate price—your life.

"Greater love has no one than this: to lay down one's life for one's friends" (John 15:13, NIV).

Be intentional. Be blessed.

# 45

I will make him a helper suitable for him.

—Genesis 2:18, NASB

Father God, we know that a husband who has a wife willing to help him fulfill Your assignments for his life has a priceless treasure. We also know that marriage is one of Your unique ways of showing both men and women that we are not sufficient by ourselves. We both need the other partner and cannot fulfill Your plans for us without their help. This is why a single mother or father struggles so desperately. Though they courageously try to be what their children need. Each role is dependent on the other's help, and it becomes impossible without Your provision for one person to perform both jobs alone. I thank You, God, for your faithful provision over my life as a single parent and that you have blessed me so that I can raise my child without a man in our home. Father, I am thankful that she has a Heavenly Father to help guide her and mold her into the beautiful young lady she will be. You are more than enough.

Be intentional. Be blessed.

# 46

I just want to take a moment to reach out my hand and be for real with all of you. I love all of you dearly.

I want you to know there is hope for anyone who has ever been through any brokenness, pain, heartbreak, abuse, etc. or who may be going through anything right now. I am a Christian, but that does not mean I am perfect nor will I ever be. I am attempting daily to be a more Christlike person, and there is nothing wrong with that. But let me also let you in on my life and let you know me a little better.

I came from a broken, abusive background. I have been in major trouble and been lovingly rebuked. I sin, and I will not judge you differently because your sins are different from mine. I have experienced heartbreak due to a spouse's infidelity. I could go on, but I communicate all of this to you to let you know that there is hope and God can shape and mold your life into something better! We lose the ability to lovingly relate to people when we present ourselves as better than anyone else. I have mad respect and sensitivity to those who have had experiences and gone through things in their lives. I am living proof that God does not leave us where he found us, and I am thankful for every painful experience as it has helped to shape and mold me into the loving work in progress I am today!

I hope you have a blessed day, and don't give up the fight!

Your past doesn't define you; God does.

Be intentional. Be blessed.

# 47

You have crowned my year with Your goodness and faithfulness. As I quickly approach another year, I want to be quick to encourage, eager to reach, and faithful to pray for my brothers and sisters. Above all, keep me growing in Your grace and knowledge in this new year as I walk hand in hand with You. In doing so, You will guide me through any dangers, for nothing can separate me from Your love that has been revealed to me through Your Son, Jesus Christ. I will remember Your steadfast love and to be thankful in all things and in all times. Though I have had unexpected storms blow in, I choose to be thankful instead of ungrateful, better instead of bitter. Every day we get to choose, and I will always choose You!

As you make your New Year's resolutions, please remember not to neglect your spiritual goals as well as your physical goals.

After all, 1 Corinthians 6:19 (NIV) says, "Your body is the Temple of The Holy Spirit."

Be intentional. Be blessed.

# 48

Are you serving God or serving man?

"Am I now trying to win the approval of men, or of God? Or am I trying to please men? If I were still trying to please men, I would not be a servant of Christ" (Gal. 1:10, NIV).

You should always put God first above man. Yes, your boyfriend, girlfriend, spouse, your children, family, etc. You are ultimately responsible for your relationship with God, and man can distract you from becoming all God wants you to be. If you find yourself too wrapped up in meeting their needs and wants, then it's time to take a step backward and reevaluate whom you are serving. When this is realized, it is up to you to correct the misplaced relationship and point them to God for support. No matter how upset they may get, how they may try to manipulate you back into it, God will see you through and will honor your decision after all God does command us to.

"But seek first his kingdom and his righteousness, and all these things will be given to you as well" (Matt. 6:33, NIV).

Be intentional. Be blessed.

# 49

Dear God,

Help me remember that I am raising someone's future wife. I am with her for such a short time. Please give me the wisdom I need to prepare her to love her husband the way you intended. Give my daughter a heart of understanding, Lord. Help her grow strong in her faith and tender in her heart. Protect her from the moral decay in this world. Plant in her the desire to seek guidance from You and to grow into a godly woman. In Jesus's name, I pray. Amen

Be intentional. Be blessed.

# 50

"Sorrowful, yet always rejoicing; poor, yet making many rich, having nothing, and yet possessing everything" (2 Cor. 6:10, NIV).

Be intentional. Be blessed.

# 51

How precious life is. This day marks the significance of more than one thing, not just the attacks on our great nation on 9/11 but the attack on my beloved nephew's life. As I stood in the delivery room helping to deliver and support my sister Romana and brother-in-love James, little Daniel was delivered. I cut the umbilical cord, and my heart sank; he was blue and not breathing. He was lifeless. I stood there for what seemed like a millennium asking God to do something. Give him life, help him to breathe, I pleaded with God. If you have ever been in a moment like this, time seems to stand still and you can't see anything or hear anything. You are just crying out to the one who gives all life—God. And in an instant, life was given. He was no longer blue, and his color came back to him. I am so thankful I got to witness this great and mighty miracle of God.

We need to open up our spiritual eyes and wake up. We are not promised tomorrow, so live each day that He gives you like it's your last. Live, laugh, love, and recognize the almighty creator God can do exceedingly and abundantly all you could ever ask for!

The word tells us in Psalm 139:13:13–16 (GWT)

> You alone created my inner being.
> You knitted me together inside my mother.
> I will give thanks to You because I have been
> so amazingly and miraculously made.
> Your words are miraculous, and
> my soul is fully aware of this.
> My bones were not hidden from You when
> I was being made in secret when I was being
> skillfully woven in an underground workshop.
> Your eyes saw me when I was only a fetus.

Every day of my life was recorded in Your
book before one of them had taken place.

I thank You, Lord, for this very valuable and precious gift of life.
May I never forget that You died so that I could live.
Be intentional. Be blessed.

# 52

Father God,

I praise You and thank you for one more birthday and one more precious year that you have given me to enjoy.

Thank you for letting me hear and experience, love and feel heartache, for the laughter and tears, joy and sorrow, I could go on. I am thankful for all of the good and the bad. I am grateful that you still perform miracles and for the miracles that I have seen this year and experienced even for myself. When I look back at the last couple of years, it has been amazing. My body was weak and failing me from being sick, but even in that weakness, you were making me strong. And my spirit is strong because of You, the one I adore, King of Kings, Lord of Lords. I refuse to focus on myself being sick when I could and am focusing on those around me who are in more need than I. I prefer to pour out Your blessings on them even if it's a little note, prayer, card, or phone call, just letting them know I care. I would rather be selfless in You, Father God, than selfish in myself.

Be intentional. Be blessed.

# 53

"Those who know your name trust in You, for You, Lord, have never forsaken those who seek you" (Ps. 9:10, NIV).

Be intentional. Be blessed.

# 54

"Let him sit alone in silence, for the Lord has laid it on him" (Lam. 3:28, NIV).

Be intentional. Be blessed.

# 55

Okay, so I have been on a fast, a spiritual fast which God released me from. I know when God calls me to fasting and praying. He has an amazing word for me, and He's about to do something big.

While on the fast, I felt like throwing up when I smelled food. He said to me, "That's how I feel when people sin. I want to vomit them out of my mouth and purge them from their destruction."

"Vomit them out of Your mouth, Lord?"

"Yes."

See, sin should make you sick and want to vomit and purge out what is not okay and honoring God. We should do our best to Honor the Holy Spirit who resides in us. After all, we were bought with a precious price: the blood of our Lord and Savior Jesus Christ.

Not only that, He had a powerful message He needed to deliver to me that I needed to be ready to receive and be in alignment with Him on. As the Lord prepares me for this incredible season, I can't help but think about our flesh against our spirit. It's amazing how distracting food can be; but when your spiritual hunger outweighs your fleshy hunger, you obey in a good way, right away and all the way. I would gladly give up a cheeseburger in exchange for some vitamin C—Christ.

Some food for thought. Are you willing?

Be intentional. Be blessed.

# 56

Cast away from you all the transgressions which you have committed, and get yourselves a new heart and a new spirit.

For I have no pleasure in the death of one who dies," says The Lord God. "Therefore turn and live!"

—Ezekiel 18:31–32, NRSV

It is not our Father's will for us to die in our sins. He loves us, and we can get a new heart and a new spirit and walk in His ways. He tells us, "You are a new creature in Christ" (2 Cor. 5:17, KJV).

You may have been knocked down, but you are not knocked out, much as a fighter gets knocked down and they count.

1. That one should be you calling on Jesus.
2. You're not through. You can do all things (Phil. 4:13, NIV).
3. Look at me. Fix your eyes on Jesus, the author and perfecter of our faith (Heb. 12:2, NIV).
4. You can endure more. Strengthened with all might, according to his glorious power, unto all patience and longsuffering with joyfulness (Col. 1:11, NIV).
5. You are still alive. I am alive with Christ (Eph. 2:5, NIV).
6. Fix. So we fix our eyes not on what is seen but on what is unseen since what is seen is temporary but what is unseen is eternal (2 Cor. 4:18, NIV).
7. Heaven. I will give you the keys of the kingdom of heaven; whatever you bind on earth will be bound in heaven, and

whatever you loose on earth will be loosed in heaven (Matt. 16:18–19, NIV).

Starting to get up.

8. Never too late. For he says, "In the time of my favor I heard you, and in the day of salvation I helped you." I tell you, now is the time of God's favor, now is the day of salvation (2 Cor. 6:2, NIV).
9. Sign. Isaiah answered, "This is the LORD's sign to you that the LORD will do what he has promised (2 Kgs. 20:9, NIV).
10. Win. Stand back to your feet. No, despite all these things, overwhelming victory is ours through Christ, who loved us (Rom. 8:37, NLT) then give God all the Glory, honor, and praise.

Our God is an awesome God.
Be intentional. Be blessed.

# 57

As I finished tonight's Bible study a sobbing mess, all I can say is wow, what an incredible journey with You Lord. Thank you to the beautiful mentor who came alongside me in this fantastic study of *In My Father's House: Finding Your Heart's True Home* by Mary A. Kassian. Your timing is perfect, as I step into the next season of my journey with you. I thank you that you gave me eyes to see, ears to hear, and a heart to obey and receive your word. May my life be a living, breathing reflection of you in all that I do and say so that others may know You and not me.

One of the exercises in the first week was to make a homemade Father's Day card expressing your heart to Him. I am being vulnerable with you and sharing my card. Your Heavenly Father is not too far away that you can't have a relationship with Him. He is waiting on you! And He has called you to a time such as this.

My card read like this:

> Father God, My sweet Daddy I want to wish you an amazing day! I honor you today. Thank you, for teaching me, shaping me, growing me. Thank you, for my intimate relationship with you. Thank you, for being there when no one else was. Thank you, for wiping my tears away and your gentle loving touch. Thank you, for loving me even when I couldn't love myself. Thank you, for never abandoning me when others did. Thank you, for restoring me, believing in me, and loving me. You have surpassed anything that I could have hoped for in a Father. I love you more and more. Thank you, for the encouragement, the

care of every detail of my life. You will forever be honored. I love you Daddy, my best friend.

You are His beloved, cherished child.
Be intentional. Be blessed.

# 58

Soldier for Christ

> Therefore put on the full armor of God, so that when the day of evil comes, you may be able to stand your ground, and after you have done everything, to stand. Stand firm then, with the belt of truth buckled around your waist, with the breastplate of righteousness in place, and with your feet fitted with the readiness that comes from the gospel of peace. In addition to all this, take up the shield of faith, with which you can extinguish all the flaming arrows of the evil one. Take the helmet of salvation and the sword of the Spirit, which is the word of God.
>
> And pray in the Spirit on all occasions with all kinds of prayers and requests. With this in mind, be alert and always keep on praying for all the Lord's people. Pray also for me, that whenever I speak, words may be given me so that I will fearlessly make known the mystery of the gospel, for which I am an ambassador in chains. Pray that I may declare it fearlessly, as I should.
> Ephesians 6:13–20 (NIV)

Every morning I wake up, I realize that I am a soldier in God's army. When I was in God's US Army, and still yet in His civilian army. I am still His soldier. I still get the honor and privilege of getting up, putting on equipment (taking up the whole armor of God), praying, and moving out on God's mission or assignment for the day. There is no greater honor than doing the work for His kingdom. Someone once asked me: Now that you are out of the army, would you really lay down your life for another? My answer is still the same as it was back then. I would gladly lay down my life for another. My missions didn't stop the day I got out of the army; it was just the beginning of what God had in store for more: His eternal army.

"Greater love has no one than this: to lay down one's life for one's friends" (John 15:13, NIV).

"We know, but do we know as we ought to know?" asked Bishop Wellington Boone in our church service.

Be intentional. Be blessed.

# 59

Ever wonder what I am up to in the middle of the night? Probably not.

Through the physical pain and discomfort, I am seeking God. I dive into the Word of God, also known as the Bible, at whatever hour. I have had five surgeries in this year alone with ongoing medical issues, but I refuse to be bitter. I will focus on an attitude of gratitude and choose to be better. I know that no matter what I am going through, God's got this!

"My soul melts from heaviness; strengthen me according to your word" (Ps. 119:28, NKJV).

God promises to encourage you in your darkest hour. If you seek Him with all of your heart, He will come to you. He will show a path that leads out of your situation. He will wipe away your tears. He will carry your heavy load. He is much better at this than you are, so let Him take it from here. Climb into His strong arms, lay your head down, and rest.

I praise God for all that He has done and all that He will do.

Be intentional. Be blessed.

# 60

God is so good! I received a post card from a member of a church I previously attended for several years. This was the note:

> On Sunday, our meditation was PS 27 The Lord is my light and my salvation whom shall I fear. (NKJV) Even though I have a banner with that on it I never thought of Him as the light to shine the fear away! May He be your light as you deal with any fears. Praying for you!

Be intentional. Be blessed.

# 61

When my daughter Latiara was seven years old, we were getting ready for church and she asked me, "Mommy, is what I am wearing honoring to God?" Then she says, "Because I want to be honoring to God." Even when they are young, we can teach our daughters and sons to be honoring God not only by their outward appearance but also their inward conduct. We are their examples, and we should be reflecting and honoring our own Heavenly Father.

Be intentional. Be blessed.

# 62

O Lord, You know all about what we encounter every day. You know the negatives that surround us at home, at work, at school, at church, in the community, and in our minds. Please remind us that if we continue to press toward You without giving up, you will surely heal and deliver us from our anguish. Help us to encourage others to lean on You when they seem discouraged by this world's troubles. Let us be an example by seeking comfort and peace in Jesus's presence. For His presence is joy beyond measure.

Be intentional. Be blessed.

# 63

I was so honored and blessed to get to be an usher tonight at the Rock Family Worship Center. What an excellent opportunity to serve God and be a blessing to His people.

Be intentional. Be blessed.

# 64

You know it's going to be an awesome day when your Heavenly Father wakes you up very early to reveal something you have been asking Him about for weeks. You reflect on your life and all of God's goodness. You hear God's beautiful creations outside waking up. The birds are chirping, the light is starting to come through. Thank you, God; I see You. I always try to pray for eyes to see, ears to hear, and a heart to obey and receive His Word. Then I ask God to give me a word. I come expectant. Same as I do in church, I pray for the same. He is always faithful and always on time.

When I amen, clap, etc., at church it's not for the pastor; it's for the Master.

Isaiah 55:1–13 is so full of wisdom.

> "Come, all you who are thirsty,
> come to the waters;
> and you who have no money,
> come, buy and eat!
> Come, buy wine and milk
> without money and without cost.
> Why spend money on what is not bread,
> and your labor on what does not satisfy?
> Listen, listen to me, and eat what is good,
> and you will delight in the richest of fare.
> Give ear and come to me;
> listen, that you may live.
> I will make an everlasting covenant with you,
> my faithful love promised to David.
> See, I have made him a witness to the peoples,
> a ruler and commander of the peoples.

Surely you will summon nations you know not,
and nations you do not know
will come running to you,
because of the LORD your God,
the Holy One of Israel,
for he has endowed you with splendor."
Seek the LORD while he may be found;
call on him while he is near.
Let the wicked forsake their ways
and the unrighteous their thoughts.
Let them turn to the LORD, and
he will have mercy on them,
and to our God, for he will freely pardon.
"For my thoughts are not your thoughts,
neither are your ways my ways,"
declares the LORD.
"As the heavens are higher than the earth,
so are my ways higher than your ways
and my thoughts than your thoughts.
As the rain and the snow
come down from heaven,
and do not return to it
without watering the earth
and making it bud and flourish,
so that it yields seed for the sower
and bread for the eater,
so is my word that goes out from my mouth:
It will not return to me empty,
but will accomplish what I desire
and achieve the purpose for which I sent it.
You will go out in joy
and be led forth in peace;
the mountains and hills
will burst into song before you,
and all the trees of the field
will clap their hands.

Instead of the thornbush will grow the juniper,
and instead of briers the myrtle will grow.
This will be for the LORD's renown,
for an everlasting sign,
that will endure forever."

Draw me nearer, Lord.

"So is my word that goes out from my mouth: It will not return to me empty, but will accomplish what I desire and achieve the purpose for which I sent it" (Isa. 55:11, NIV).

Be intentional. Be blessed.

# 65

When God guides, He provides. Simple but profound!
Be intentional. Be blessed.

# 66

Lord God, where would I be without your love? A love that not only shelters me in the height of the storm but helps me grow and thrive no matter the weather. Help me to remember that no matter what is going on, You are still in the midst.

Be intentional. Be blessed.

# 67

Give us, we pray to you, almighty God, a mind forgetful of past injury, a will to seek the good of others, and a heart of love.

Be intentional. Be blessed.

# 68

Jesus, help me to see the humor in everyday occurrences. And when I make mistakes, remind me it isn't the end of the world. It's a learning experience, an opportunity to laugh and to trust Your sovereignty.

Be intentional. Be blessed.

# 69

It is God who works in you to will and to act according to His good purpose" (Phil. 2:13, NIV).

Be intentional. Be blessed.

# 70

Are you dealing with someone whom you feel will never change? Do you vacillate between wishing he/she would change and just wanting him/her to leave you alone? Have you given up expecting good things from that person? Nobody is so far from God that he/she can't get back to the Lord. Our responsibility is to keep knocking at God's door about that person, to keep believing God will answer our prayers. Thank God for what He will do. Patiently but expectantly wait on the Lord. Renew your hope!

Be intentional. Be blessed.

# 71

"For God so loved the world he gave his only begotten son that who-soever believe in him should not perish but have everlasting life" (John 3:16, NIV).

What does this mean? I can't even fathom the amount of sac-rifice and love of God to send His only Son into this sin-stricken world. But why did He send Him? He knew, Father God El Roi, what we needed. What were we in need of? A Savior.

See, God loved us so much that He would sacrifice His Son Jesus's life on the cross because we are sinners. He interceded on our behalf taking every sin to the cross, and there it was nailed. Jesus fin-ished what we could never do.

It is God's desire for no one to perish but have everlasting life, and that can start today. Right here.

Say, "Lord Jesus, come into my heart, cleanse me of my sins. I know that my sins have separated me from you. Lord, please forgive me of my iniquities and help me to live a life honoring to you. I believe that Your Son died for my sins, my wickedness, and He was brought back from the dead, is alive, and hears my prayer. I invite You, Jesus, to be the Lord of my life. Reign in my heart from this day forward, Lord, and please send your Holy Spirit to help me obey You and do Your will for the rest of my life. In Jesus's name, I pray. Amen."

He desires a personal relationship with you, one day at a time, one step at a time. When He encounters you, your life will never be the same!

Be intentional. Be blessed.

# 72

I am reminded of Jeremiah 18.

> This is the word that came to Jeremiah from the Lord: "Go down to the potter's house, and there I will give you my message." So I went down to the potter's house, and I saw him working at the wheel. But the pot he was shaping from the clay was marred in his hands; so the potter formed it into another pot, shaping it as seemed best to him. (Jer. 18:1–4, NIV)

This is much like me and my life. I was marred with His hands, and the Lord formed me into something else, shaping me as it seemed best to Him.

I thank you, Father, that I have the freedom to humbly and boldly proclaim what you have done for me and my life. I know if you can do it for me, you can do it for so many others. Lord, let my life be a witness to so many nonbelievers and believers that you are a forgiving God and that our past does not define us. That we can boldly and confidently step into our destinies that you have set us apart for. Lord, I thank you for the call on my life and the many generations before me and after me.

Lord, for many days you know I wept because I was over-whelmed by your love and still am. I still ask who am I that I would find favor in your sight? And you still answer me just the same. "You are my beloved, beautiful, cherished, and loved daughter."

I know who I am. I am yours

Be intentional. Be blessed.

# 73

Okay, this one is long, but maybe this will help or be a blessing to someone today.

Are you suited up? Whether you are working in a lab, going to ride a bicycle, playing football, going scuba diving, going to work, going out to the grocery store, going to church, being a soldier, and so much more, are you suited up? This is a question we must ask ourselves. And if so, am I completely ready?

After all, I don't think I would be considered completely ready if I am missing a piece of my clothing, suit, gear, or armor, more specifically, the armor of God.

So how about this, when we are getting ready in the morning, as quickly as it is to put on a piece of clothing, at the same time put on the armor of God. Yes, literally put it on. There is power in our words, followed by actions, sealed by the Lord in prayer.

Watch out, devil! Today will not be the day because this is the day that the Lord hath made and I will rejoice and be glad in it.

Ephesians 6:13–20 (NIV) tells you exactly how to do it, all of it. "Gird your waist with truth, put on the breastplate of righteousness, shod your feet with the preparation of the gospel of peace, take the shield of faith, take the helmet of salvation, and the sword of the Spirit, the word of God; praying with all prayer and supplication in the Spirit, being watchful."

This is for males or females.

1. So let us look at what *gird* means: secure (a garment or sword) on the body with a belt or band. As I put on my totally stylish belt, I gird my waist in truth.
2. I put on my breastplate of righteousness. My cute blouse, T-shirt, tank top, button up, this is even for the guys.

Whatever I am wearing, I am remembering that what I am wearing is totally a reflection of Christ. So I honor Him by covering up what belongs to Him, or if I have a husband what belongs to him as well. After all, my body is the temple of the Holy Spirit and should be treated as such (1 Cor. 6:19, NIV). I can't stress enough holiness, purity, spotlessness. Not to mention how awkward you would feel if Christ let it all hang out. Just being for real, I don't think so. How awkward, I am just saying; on that note moving on.

3. Shod, referring to shoe of a person by wearing shoes of a particular kind. Your feet with the preparation of the gospel of peace. So I pick out my specific type of shoe whether it be flats, boots, heels, tennis shoes, etc., and proclaim peace and ask Him to order my steps in Jesus's name!

4. Take the shield of faith. I literally simulate grabbing up my shield of faith as a mighty warrior.

5. The helmet of salvation. I put it on even if no one can see it. I wear a crown because I know who I am in Christ. I am a daughter of the highest, and that makes me a princess. I have been bought with a heavenly price, and He thinks I am to die for. We all should know our precious identity in Him so that in His strength we can be the change that we want to see in this world. It starts at home, one day at a time, one step at a time. This crazy life we live is a process of beautiful or handsome refinement.

6. And finally, the sword of the Spirit, the Word of God. I literally lift my Bible to the heavens, and I say, "I thank you, Lord, that you have given me all of your spiritual armor, and I thank you that you have hidden your Word in my heart so that I may use it as I face this day. I thank you, God, that I may open my mouth boldly and confidently in You, Lord God, to make known the mystery of the gospel, for which I am an ambassador in chains so that I can speak boldly as I ought to speak about You. In Jesus's mighty name, I pray. Amen.

Be intentional. Be blessed.

# 74

Now all glory to God, who is able, through His mighty power at work within us, to accomplish infinitely more than we might ask or think.

—Ephesians 3:20, NLT

Immeasurable love and unending forgiveness are characteristics that only God can give so freely so much so that even the most appalling wrongdoer who believes will be pardoned. Because of Your great and outstanding example of affection and compassion toward us, we can also extend the same toward others. As receivers of Your goodness, may we be dispersers of Your blessings to those You bring into our lives.

Be intentional. Be blessed.

# 75

He who sows to his flesh will…reap corruption, but he who sows to the Spirit will reap everlasting life.

—Galatians 6:8, NKJV

Life is full of trade-offs. Today's bad choices are a down payment for tomorrow's problems. It's all part of living and understanding the law of God that says we reap what we sow (Gal. 6:7, NKJV). This being true of a friend who got a felony conviction for drinking and driving that resulted in a fifteen-year prison sentence. The judge then suspended fourteen years of the sentence if the friend would honor the terms of a one-year house arrest. The trade-off was pretty simple in nature. Stay at home and out of trouble for one year instead of going to prison for fifteen. But the friend didn't like being stuck in the house, so the friend went and did what they wanted, driving on a suspended license to get there. The friend was arrested again, and the judge put the friend in prison. Those trips cost the friend many years of freedom.

What bad trade-offs do we make?

Do we reject God's mercy so we can enjoy sin's season of pleasure? In the Bible, we see examples of trade-offs. Moses traded the Promised Land for an outburst of anger (Num. 20:7–13, NKJV). David traded his reputation for a night of passion (2 Sam. 11, NKJV). Ananias and Sapphira traded life for some extra money (Acts 5:1–11, NKJV).

Are you facing temptation today? Don't give in. Cling to Christ. Obey His commands.

It has been said by Dave Brannon, "Never exchange fellowship with Him for anything. It's always a poor trade-off."

It's wise to flee when tempted.

A fool is one who'd stay;
For those who toy with evil
Soon learn it doesn't pay.

(D. De Haan)

Be intentional. Be blessed.

# 76

The Lord is good to those who wait for Him,
To the soul who seeks Him.
It is good that one should hope and wait quietly
For the salvation of The Lord.

—Lamentations 3:25–26, NKJV

Ever been in a crisis and seen someone freaking out? They are all over the place and don't know which way is up or down, or what to do. They are what you call "beside themselves."

As Christians, when a crisis comes our way, we don't have to freak out because God has equipped us with all we ever need, to respond instead of reacting. How awesome is that?

As it says in the above scripture, "The Lord is good to those who wait for Him." To the soul who seeks Him. How much more help can He be to us? He is telling us to expect. "Don't freak out." Seek Him. Pray about it. Ask Him what to do. You already know He says He will direct our path, so "hope and wait quietly... and He will come." God's got this! Whatever this is, He already knows. Remember He not only sees me, He sees you as well. Just as I can freely call on His magnificent and precious name so can you.

Be intentional. Be blessed.

# 77

And this same God who takes care of me will supply all your needs from his glorious riches, which have been given to us in Christ Jesus.

—Philippians 4:19, NLT

Father God,

I thank you that You are my portion and inheritance. You are faithful. I can count on You. You have always been committed to keeping Your word. You have supplied all my needs. Most of the time, I have much more than I could ever use or appreciate. So often, Your provisions get doubted when there is the confusion of needs versus wants. I want to take this time to thank you for giving me all I need, and my wants too. I know I don't deserve anything, and it's by Your grace that I can receive what you have given me.

I am with a thankful heart.

Be intentional. Be blessed.

# 78

I love spending time with this lady, a mighty warrior, an awesome woman of God!

Nicholette Scott challenges me in ways I never thought possible. She is one of my best friends who is not afraid to tell me the truth no matter what it looks like. I love that she is not my yes friend. She doesn't tell me what I want to hear. Everyone needs true friends. They tell you the hard but loving stuff. They will pray for you, and they are rooted and grounded in love. And in His name is Jesus.

"Don't ever let me get so Christian I lose my faith," said Nicholette Scott.

Be intentional. Be blessed.

# 79

An older gentleman failed to yield to oncoming traffic then preceded to put his window down to cuss me out when I swerved to miss him. All I said was, "God Bless you, brother. I will be praying for you." Thank you, God, I am not who I was before.

Be intentional. Be blessed.

# 80

While sitting at Valley Imaging Center in Athens today to get an MRI done, I got to share the love Jesus Christ has so freely given to me with an individual. It's so beautiful and honoring that He uses us to carry out His will. What is also exciting was that I was led to be there early, an hour early even though I didn't know why. I knew I needed to listen. His timing is perfect! He is so good!

Be intentional. Be blessed.

# 81

O Lord, as I think about joy and fun, I am reminded of 1 Timothy 6:17 (NIV) that instructs us not to trust in the uncertainty of wealth but to put our hope in God who richly provides us with everything for our enjoyment. Thank you for the laughter You create in the fellowship of being together with those we love. It is a gift of Your grace.

Be intentional. Be blessed.

# 82

Happy moments, praise God. Difficult moments, seek God. Quiet moments, worship God. Painful moments, trust God. Every moment, thank God.

Be intentional. Be blessed.

# 83

The past should be put behind you and not be an everlasting punishment. What's done is done. Constantly going over the ordeals you previously faced will only be a burden in your life. Unless you let God use your story for His glory, then as He turns your pain into purpose and you get healing, He allows you to tell your once painful story again to help someone else who is going through the same things you did. It is up to us to pursue our own healing.

In the end, He puts His stamp on your past. You are the healed of the Lord, redeemed of the Lord, and loved of the Lord.

If He can do it for me, He can do it for you!

Be intentional. Be blessed.

# 84

"Bear with each other and forgive whatever grievances you may have against one another. Forgive as the Lord forgave you" (Col. 3:13, NIV).

Be intentional. Be blessed.

# 85

Lord, I want to bless You with praise for Your gift of forgiveness given through Your Son Jesus Christ. Your marvelous love has set me free from the guilt and consequences of my sin. Because You are loving, You are forgiving. I rejoice and am humbled by Your abundant forgiveness.

Be intentional. Be blessed.

# 86

"Love is patient; love is kind. It does not envy; it does not boast, it is not proud. It is not rude; it is not self-seeking, it is not easily angered, it keeps no record of wrongs. Love does not delight in evil but rejoices with the truth. It always protects, always trusts, always hopes, always perseveres. Love never fails" (1 Cor. 13:4–8, NIV).

Be intentional. Be blessed.

# 87

From Sarah McClain:

You know I never used to. Until I met this outstanding woman of God, who is a beautiful and wonderfully made woman of God! Cristy Castleberry is her name. One day I gained the courage to get to know more mom's in my SHE Mom's group at church (if you're not familiar with what it's about Just pm me and I'll let ya know). So we hung out for around 4-5 hours just talking about who we were and who our families were. It was so amazing! It felt as if we had known each other for years; that's how comfortable it felt to talk with my sister in Christ. She made you feel loved and like you belonged in the world. After that one day of hanging out with her, I became so passionate in my "talks" with God while in the car. I grew so much in my relationship with Him that day that praying in the car just became second nature lol. Telling our Lord Almighty how my day was going and thanking Him for all His blessings. Even just getting home safely or to another destination safely was a blessing. Our time is not promised in this world, so I'd rather live it in by the Spirit than of my flesh. If you don't know what that means I recommend you get the book Holy Spirit by John Bevere. It's so amazing! I like to do it over and over just to renew my Spirit in Christ. Anyways back on track. Lol, Cristy, I thank you so much for loving me as a friend and most of all a sister. You're relationship with the Holy Spirit, Jesus, and God is one I'm working on having. God had a purpose and a timing for us that day, and I thank Him for it so much. Never stop being who you are! You move mountains!

Be intentional. Be blessed.

# 88

Everything that God filters to come our way is always with purpose. He uses even the greatest error and deepest pain to mold us into a better person.

Be intentional. Be blessed.

# 89

An answered prayer arrived today.

I have trigeminal neuralgia, which is a nerve disorder in my face. It only affects the right side and includes my eye, ear, jaw, throat, neck, and the right side of my head. It's excruciating and makes me extremely sick. I had to go to the ER today because the pain was no longer manageable. I have been dealing with this for a long time now. Ever since I was a child, getting hit and slapped in my face as discipline caused the painful effects that have lasted for years. The nurse who came in has the same thing, and she has referred me to a pain specialist about it. She said they give her a shot to block the pain in the nerve and has been pain-free for about a year. I have been praying for help with this matter.

Thank You, God, for Your faithful provision and placing the nurse in my path.

Be intentional. Be blessed

# 90

God is so amazing! Today, I had to go to the pain clinic; and the people there were so amazing, sweet, understanding, and so full of the presence of the Lord. And we talked about God and the amazing things that He has done. From that time in the ER when God placed that beautiful nurse in my path who has trigeminal neuralgia too, to today and my encounter in the pain clinic. I am so in awe of His protection and provision over my life. He is always faithful and on time.

On that following Monday, I went in to be put under for the nerve block procedure for the first time.

Be intentional. Be blessed.

# 91

I went in for another procedure this morning for my trigeminal neuralgia. It's excruciating as it is, and they had to inject medicine by needle into my face and behind my ear, which hurts too. I am praying that I will be able to attend FAB Friday at my church tonight.

Update from today's procedure. My face is pretty swollen on the right side, and I have some weird numbness I haven't experienced before with my face and mouth. But I will wait and see if it is better tomorrow. Minor pain right now, which is awesome considering the procedure. I will be at FAB Friday! I'm not going to let this get in the way. Ice pack and all. God is so good!

Be intentional. Be blessed

# 92

Going in for my injections again today. Feeling anxious.

"Do not be anxious about anything, but in every situation, by prayer and petition, with thanksgiving, present your requests to God" (Phil. 4:6, NIV).

As many times as I have prayed and submitted this to Him in the last few hours, He is probably like, "I hear you already."

God is good all the time.

Be intentional. Be blessed

# 93

The other day, I was supposed to get my facial injections. They have messed up my appointment for my injections. Apparently, they even scheduled me for the wrong procedure.

Last time, it took four months to get in when they had a similar issue. Please pray for the Lord's continued and renewed strength while I continue to endure this long suffering. I am trying to count it all as joy, but today is a rough day when I have already waited a couple of months and I live with the pain on a daily basis. Just being real.

Be intentional. Be blessed.

# 94

Okay, the procedure went well. I am praising God for answered prayers. They had to give me morphine on top of the injections due to the pain. I am experiencing numbness in my lips and mouth and feeling nauseated when standing, but I am finally home and working on getting myself around to go to church and praise God! A huge thank you to all who have lifted me up in prayer and supported me through all of this. No words can describe how humbled and thankful I am to have you as my sisters and brothers as well as call you my friends. The texts, phone calls, and emails mean so much to me.

With a humble heart, I say thank you. I love you all.

Be intentional. Be blessed

# 95

In September of 2015 at the SHE IS Brave conference at The Rock Family Worship Center in Huntsville, I shared part of my testimony. I have trigeminal neuralgia, also known as suicide disease, and this is what it looked like. What is the point of these pictures? It's to give hope and a future to the generations who went before me and coming behind me. To know that we serve a God who is bigger than our current circumstances. The God I serve is more than the pain and long suffering I had endured. In fact, He tells us in His Word: "Not only that, but we rejoice in our sufferings, knowing that suffering produces endurance, and endurance produces character, and character produces hope, and hope does not put us to shame, because God's love has been poured into our hearts through the Holy Spirit who has been given to us" (Rom. 5:3–5, ESV).

When I got three shots in my face on a Wednesday, I still showed up for the church service. I say all of this not to glorify me in any way, shape, or form as my righteousness is filthy rags but to tell you all about the God I serve. Did I want to come to church? My flesh would say, "No Way! Are you crazy?" My flesh wanted to stay at home and do absolutely nothing.

The Holy Spirit that resides in me because I commune with Him daily said, "Your flesh is weak, but My Spirit is strong in you. And your flesh may fail, but I'm your God and I never will." So I died to my flesh. I put on my full armor, the full armor of God (Eph. 6:13–24, NIV), got dressed, fixed my hair, added a little makeup. And went on assignment. So my point in all of this is, my God is bigger and if I fix my eyes on Jesus instead of my pain—the distraction—and my spirit is in right standing with the Lord, I can command my flesh to get in line with my Spirit. And it does. Because "greater is He, who is in me than he who is in the world" (1 John 4:4,

NIV). No matter what situation I face, He has already equipped me with all I will ever need, and this I am sure. I will remain confident in Him. I will see the goodness of the Lord.

Be intentional. Be blessed.

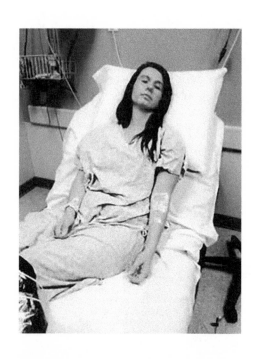

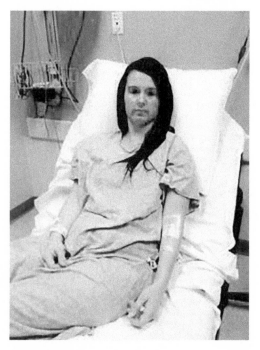

SHE IS BRAVE -Women's Conference Photo Shoot-I had received my shots in the right side of my face that day so, I could not have warrior paint on the right side. If you look carefully you can tell that my right side of my face is swollen.

# 96

About eight months later, this was my testimony.

As I woke up this morning without the extreme pain, I am thankful. Those who know my story know it has been a long journey dealing with the nerve disorder on the right side of my face. I just wanted to share something great God has done for me. When people would tell me to go up for prayer and healing, I had no problem as long as the Holy Spirit was prompting me. When people would say to me, "You are not healed due to your lack of faith," I would say, "Oh honey let, me tell you what my faith in the Father can do. It can move mountains." And then I would share God's amazing testimonies about it and what God did as a result of my faith in Him.

It's always God, never me. When there would be an altar call about healing, people would say to me, "You need to go."

I would say to them, "Why? I am already healed, I have already boldly claimed that promise. The Lord tells us by *His* stripes we are healed, *He* doesn't tell you on which side *He* is going to manifest it. And I believed and received my healing in faith in *Him*."

It's a spiritual maturity and understanding most people can't understand unless they have experienced it themselves when healing doesn't look like what we think it should then we tend to discount it. A great mystery He has revealed to me. So in my post on Facebook I said, "I say all of this to share with you that a couple of months ago in which I am just now being released to tell you all that the Lord has told me, 'YOUR FAITH HAS MADE YOU WELL.' So, as I went in and got my shots this last time months ago, it was distinctly different than any other, I woke up early in recovery, I asked them is it time to go, and the lady said no, 'we haven't even finished your paperwork.' Usually, they have to wake me up. Lol."

I also asked for less pain medicine. When I asked, she said, "Less pain medicine? What do you mean? We have never had a patient ask for less pain medicine. But we'll do it." I didn't have nausea and experience throwing up like I did every time before.

He also said, "Push your injections back to four months and watch what I can do." Those who know about this trigeminal neuralgia know it is excruciating, and I had battled it daily.

I had to get three shots into my face every two months, and in between, I would end up in the ER having to get demerol shots to take the edge off the pain, and throwing up.

I boldly and confidently say in Christ to everyone once again that I am healed in Jesus's name!

My pain wasn't even close to what Christ had to endure; I am sure. But I do have a reality of what long-suffering is, and I can't help but remember to be thankful and reflect on how much God went through for me, suffering in pain and agony to the point of His death.

If He can do it for me, He can do it for you.

Keep your eyes fixed on Jesus.

Be intentional. Be blessed.

# 97

"We glory in tribulation, knowing that tribulation produces perseverance" (Rom. 5:3, ESV).

Have you ever been a complainer at some point? I know I have. Have you ever felt that your complaining was justified? After all, did I really ask for all the pain and frustration that I go through at times? Certainly not, thought I. But God thought differently. The Lord knows just what I need to grow and change spiritually. In Romans 5:3–4, Paul teaches that life's problems can produce godly character in us.

My complaining hinders God's work.

Here are some advice to overcome a complaining attitude.

1. Know that God is in control. Your troubles do not surprise Him.
2. Believe and have faith that God has the resolution, provision, or a gift of wisdom that He is willing to give to match your hardship.
3. Pray and affirm who you are in Him. Express your confidence in Him and acknowledge His perfect love and purpose for you.
4. Wait, expect, be available, and trust God to work out His perfect plan for you, not your earthly plan.
5. Praise Him even before He acts.

These alternatives to complaining give God an opportunity to work in His own unique way, both in us and in our situations. Best of all, even if your situation doesn't change, rest assured that He is using it to change you!

Don't complain about the thorns among roses; be grateful for the roses among thorns.

I love it when God gives me revelations and understandings about my life and my situations.

Be intentional. Be blessed.

# 98

For we are God's [own] handiwork (His work-manship), recreated in Christ Jesus, [born anew] that we may do those good works which God predestined (planned beforehand) for us [taking paths which He prepared ahead of time], that we should walk in them [living the good life which He prearranged and made ready for us to live.]

—Ephesians 2:10, AMPC

God doesn't make mistakes. He is the perfect planner.

I am recently reminded that He is the perfect planner; I am not. Anyone who knows me knows I prefer to plan things, prepare, etc. I was getting ready for the life group God has called me to teach on Thursdays, and as I was upstairs getting ready, time slipped further and further away from me. So I was having this argument with God about how I need to be downstairs preparing. I finally got downstairs, and there was maybe five to ten minutes before everyone showed up. So I was like, "Okay, I got this."

The next thing that happened was that the DVD remote was nowhere to be found. By that time, I should have freaked out, right? People are already showing up. And it dawned on me that God had a different plan for our life group and me. So I tell everyone God had a different plan for us that night. We have to be able to let go and let God. If I had freaked out when I couldn't find the DVD remote, got all upset because things didn't go according to my plan, there was a huge possibility He wouldn't have been able to use me. I would have dishonored Him on so many different levels with my speech, actions, etc. But because I have an intimate relationship with my Heavenly

Father and I know when He is speaking to me, I can set aside my plan for my Father's perfect plan. I love Him more than anything, and I rejoice that He loves me enough to change my earthly plan into His heavenly plan.

God makes all things work together for my good.

I am overwhelmed and humbled that God would use me to impact others' lives for His kingdom, and there is no greater honor. I am so thankful!

Remember, it's always Him not me.

My prayer is for you to be encouraged in the Lord.

Be intentional. Be blessed.

# 99

And I am convinced and sure of this very thing, that He who began a good work in you will continue until the day of Jesus Christ [right up to the time of His return], developing [that good work] and perfecting and bringing it to full completion in you.

—Philippians 1:6, AMPC

We know ourselves better than any human being. We can immediately recall all of our failures or shortcomings. Satan would love for us to continually rehearse these things and not believe the word quoted above from Philippians. The plan isn't perfect because we're perfect; it's because God is perfect. God has a particular and unique plan for each one of our lives who believes in Him and receives Him to bring honor and glory to His kingdom.

Don't discredit yourself due to past failures, to something someone spoke over your life, your current circumstances, etc.

He is able. He doesn't wait around for us to get qualified or wait on us to feel good enough about ourselves to feel worthy enough to do His work.

If you are a Christian, you better suit up. Put on the full armor of God and be ready because He has called *you* for a time such as this.

Be intentional. Be blessed.

# 100

Who shall separate us from the love of Christ? Shall trouble or hardship or persecution or famine or nakedness or danger or sword? No, in all these things we are more than conquerors through Him who loved us.

—Romans 8:35, 37, NIV

Be strong in the Lord, and He will get you through the storm. Be intentional. Be blessed.

# 101

Remember who your real Valentine is—God! What is God? He is love. Be intentional. Be blessed.

# 102

On a Wednesday night, Pastor Chris Mitchell brought the word.

> The Lord convicted (notice I didn't say condemned) me of something that happened over fifteen years ago. I had to repent and apologize. When you ask God to see others as He does; be ready. So thankful, that He provided that opportunity, and for the ability to feel true godly sorrow for what I had done, and apologize sincerely. He continues to soften my heart in ways I never thought possible. Thank you, God, for your faithful provision even when I need to be corrected. Nothing like a real loving Father to do the correcting.

Be intentional. Be blessed.

# 103

For as he thinks in his heart, so is he.

—Proverbs 23:7, NKJV

Whatever we focus on, we become. If you are negative, examine your thought life. You may find without knowing that you are feeding those thoughts based on your emotions. Choosing our thoughts wisely helps us to maintain a joyful godly life and does not allow an open door for the enemy to come in. Guard the gates of your heart. Read the Word over and over until it becomes a reality. You may not feel it at the time, but you can be sure you are feeding your spirit. And the more you feed your spirit, the flesh will die, and you will find yourself more joyful, kind, patient, equipped with all those fruits of the spirit. Don't speak negative things over your life and never allow someone else to do it either. Rebuke it in the name of Jesus and keep going. God is the one who defines you, not man.

Remember you are very valuable, beautiful, handsome, and loved. Gotta cover the men as well as this applies to them too. And yes, men do have emotions.

Be intentional. Be blessed.

# 104

I will give you a new heart, and a new spirit I will put within you. And I will remove the heart of stone from your flesh and give you a heart of flesh. And I will put my Spirit within you, and cause you to walk in my statutes and be careful to obey my rules.

—Ezekiel 36:26–28, NIV

The right heart is not the result of human effort. It is the gift of God and the work of His Holy Spirit in the life of the person.

Thank you, God, that you have removed my heart of stone and given me a heart of flesh.

I have had to walk this one out myself in my life due to things that have happened to me. I am living proof that God can take a mess and turn it into a message that would bring life to others. It is only through God in me that I can be truly transformed by His love, grace, and forgiveness. I am so thankful He did not leave me where He found me.

Be intentional. Be blessed.

# 105

Lord, I am not perfect as you know, but I am so thankful that You still love me even when I fail, forgive me, help me brush off my knees, put the Band-aid on, and help me get back on my feet even when others do not. You are the only failproof plan, and You are the only thing I need.

Be intentional. Be blessed.

# 106

"The Lord is my portion, says my soul, "Therefore I hope in Him!"

—Lamentations 3:24, NKJV

You lay your head on your pillow tonight and know it's been a terrible day. Your sin got the best of you all day long. Where did your self-control go? Guilt and shame begin to swallow you. You feel so far away from God. He must really be disappointed, you think. All you want to do is hide, Hide from your friends and yourself but mostly from God. But the right thing to do is to run to Him. He is tender and loving. His forgiveness is pure and cleansing. His compassion brings comfort. His mercy grants freedom. His loving kindness lets you open your eyes in the morning and be glad for the new day. It's a start-over day. It's a clean-slate day. It's a new day, with new compassion from the God of new beginnings.

Be intentional. Be blessed.

# 107

Dear Lord Jesus, there's so much in life that isn't fun, that hurts and drags us down. Give us the eyes to focus on the stray joys that could so easily slip past us. Help us widen our vision to not only encompass those comfort breaks but to see how we can bring comfort to others in whatever stage of life we may be.

Be intentional. Be blessed.

# 108

Lord, what a risk you took on loving us. Give us wisdom and courage to risk loving you in return.

Be intentional. Be blessed.

# 109

Father, Your warnings regarding the deceitful tactics of the enemy are evidenced all around us through the social media, books, false prophets, and even well-meaning but confused individuals. Your Word is our stability needed for life. Help us to obtain Your godly wisdom, be studied, and alert so that we can correctly discern good from evil, truth from lies.

Be intentional. Be blessed.

# 110

When you go with God to a new level, you get a new level of the devil. The devil wouldn't be coming after you if you weren't a threat. Be intentional. Be blessed.

# 111

No temptation (no trial regarded as enticing to sin), (no matter how it comes or where it leads) has overtaken you and laid hold on you that is not common to man (that is, no temptation or trial has come to you that is beyond human resistance, and this is not adjusted and adopted and belonging to human experience, and such as man can bear). But God is faithful (to his word and to His compassionate nature), and He (can be trusted) not to let you be tempted and tried beyond your ability and strength of resistance and power to endure, but with the temptation He will (always) also provide the way out (The means of escape to a landing place), that you may be capable and strong and powerful to bear up under it patiently.

—1 Corinthians 10:13, AMPC

We don't have the right to guilt or shift blame to other people or circumstances for our behavior. We can't use them as an excuse to stay in bondage. Christ came to set us free.

Be intentional. Be blessed.

# 112

When God wakes you up at four in the morning to read *The Bait of Satan* by John Bevere, you know He's got a real message for you.

Don't let anyone affect your relationship with God.

Here I am, Lord.

Obedience is better than sacrifice.

Be intentional. Be blessed.

# 113

From Angelique:

> I just had the most wonderful birthday dinner
> with one of my best friends God has placed in my
> life. She is so amazing, His presence was there.
> Just talking about how good He is an how we
> are growing in Him. I think of her as my men-
> tor. When I see her I see a better view of Jesus
> and how He uses her and her obedience when He
> tells her things to do. All I want is to know You
> more Lord, hear your sweet voice and serve you
> wholeheartedly.

Be intentional. Be blessed.

# 114

Quote from my daughter today (she is referring to the Ashley Scott testimony):

> Geez, mom, you are like God's mailman. Giving people good news and the good news happens. I mean geez. Me: Um it's ALL God, not me!
>
> I am just obedient to what He tells me even if it seems crazy to the natural He confirms it in the spiritual. Giving God ALL the glory, honor, and praise. What an honor to be called God's mailman.
>
> There is no greater honor in this lifetime than to do the work for God's kingdom.

Be intentional. Be blessed.

# 115

Saturday, January 16, 2016, 4:06 p.m. was an amazing day, a day that would forever impact my life, faith, and my relationship with our Lord and Savior Jesus Christ. It was the last day of the Championship Summit conference, and as I stood in the sanctuary, the Lord spoke to me about the message He wanted me to deliver. I argued and wrestled with my flesh and with God about how crazy I am going to look if I let someone know that the Lord had had me praying over their womb and pregnancy, and that they were barren but the Lord has restored them. I finally said, "Okay, Lord, I'll do it. I will take the risk. At the expense of looking crazy for You, I will do it." Keep in mind I didn't know why God had me praying over Mrs. Ashley Ransburg Scott's womb and the details regarding her condition, so at 4:06 p.m., I sent a text to her. My heart raced.

I texted and told her what the Lord had said to me. "Hi Ashley-This is going to sound crazy but The Lord has been speaking to me now several times now about pregnancy for you. He has had me praying over your womb. Your womb was barren, but He has restored you! Just like Elisabeth. He hears your prayers, your cries, If you are not pregnant now, you will be!

"Praise God for His Faithfulness!!! Love you sister!"

Be intentional. Be blessed.

# 116

There was no immediate response, so I thought in my flesh for a brief moment, *Oh no, now I am the crazy person.* But wait for it. Ashley's response to my text:

> Thank you for being obedient to the Holy Spirit!!! I am in tears because my husband and I have been struggling to get pregnant for almost two years!!
>
> I am overwhelmed because I was diagnosed with PCOS and I believe I was healed at SheRev!
>
> When Alex Seeley preached on the woman with the issue of blood, she called up women with different afflictions, and God had her call out MY issue!!!!
>
> We found out on Christmas Eve that we ARE pregnant!
>
> Blood tests were positive, and we have our first ultrasound on MONDAY!!
>
> What a blessing YOU are! I continue to cry because God is SO good. I am so thankful for your obedience and your heart.

Me:

> Reading this I immediately shouted for Joy and praised God!!!! Thank you for your faithfulness and sharing your testimony with me! I don't always know why He has me praying for people and specifics. This is an amazing testimony for the kingdom of God!!! I give God ALL the Glory,

Honor, and Praise!!! I just know I love Him and want to be sensitive to Him and obedient! I love you, sister!!!

He just keeps confirming to my spirit don't ever doubt you hear from me!!! He's a Good Good Father

# 117

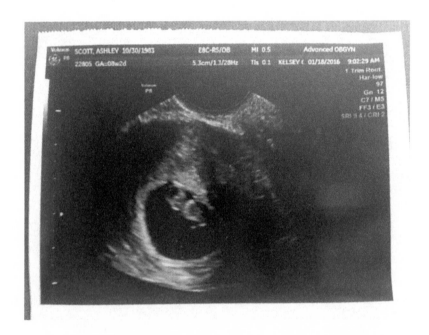

January 18, 2016. Their tiny angel baby was confirmed on
ultrasound. Faith Elise, this child Ashley and Cordell Scott
had prayed for. The promise was spoken and given.

The Lord says in John 14:12–14 (NLT), "I tell you the truth, anyone
who believes in me will do the same works I have done, and even
greater works, because I am going to be with the Father. You can ask
for anything in my name, and I will do it, so that the Son can bring
glory to the Father. Yes, ask me for anything in my name, and I will
do it!"

Amazing Faith!

Faith Elise was born August 12, 2016.

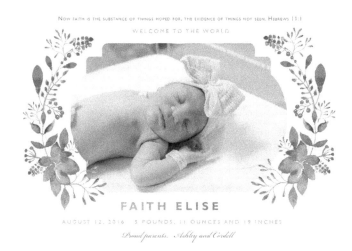

Now faith is the substance of things hoped for, the evidence of things not seen. Hebrews 11:1

WELCOME TO THE WORLD

FAITH ELISE

AUGUST 12, 2016  5 POUNDS, 11 OUNCES AND 19 INCHES

Proud parents, Ashley and Cordell

Out of a steadfast, unwavering faith, God gave them the child they asked for in prayer.

There is no greater honor in this lifetime than to do the work for His kingdom, to be used as a vessel for Christ's kingdom and to watch a miracle unfold on this side of the earth. To God be *all* the glory, honor, and praise.

To Ashley and Cordell, with a humble heart, I thank you for your faithfulness before Christ and His church and for allowing me to share your amazing testimony of God's faithfulness. I love you both!

Be intentional. Be blessed.

# 118

Praising God, I woke up this morning and God answered my prayer! Off to Elijah House 202 School of Prayer Ministry I go! I come expectant and hungry for you, Lord!

Thank you for your faithful provision!

Be intentional. Be blessed.

# 119

"But Samuel replied, 'What is more pleasing to the LORD: your burnt offerings and sacrifices or your obedience to his voice? Listen! Obedience is better than sacrifice, and submission is better than offering the fat of rams.'" (1 Sam. 15:22, NLT)

Be intentional. Be blessed.

# 120

So today marks a significant intimate milestone in my life. I have completed reading His Word for the very first time, a journey I started many years ago, an estimated over 1,095 days ago with my Lord and Savior Jesus Christ. I couldn't be more honored to close out my year with my Heavenly Father being closer than my daughter, my mother, my sister, my brother, or my friends. Paul said it best in Philippians 3:12 (NIV): "Not that I have already obtained all this, or have already arrived at my goal, but I press on to take hold of that for which Christ Jesus took hold of me."

I am thankful for His amazing revelations He has given to me and friendship on this journey called life. I give Him *all* the glory, honor, and praise.

I look forward to the incredible journey God will lead me on in the years to come.

Be intentional. Be blessed.

# 121

We love because He first Loved us.

—1 John 4:19, NIV

I can't describe the gut-wrenching feeling of almost missing this opportunity for us to bless this eleven-year-old. Looking at the Christmas tree that contained the Kids to Love children, there were only a few left on Sunday during the third service, and they were the older kids whose items were a bit more expensive. I was looking, and I almost walked away when the Lord spoke to me. "What are you doing?"

"Well they are all expensive, we can't afford this."

"Who provides for you?"

"But... no... but."

"Where does your help come from?"

"You, God. Okay, Father, I am going to be obedient and do what you ask. I am trusting you. You've never let me down." Needless to say not only did the Lord show up and show out, but He also provided more than was asked on the ornament, a better system and at a lower price.

Obedience is better than sacrifice.

Our God is an awesome God!

Be intentional. Be blessed.

# 122

God is a rewarder to those who diligently seek Him.

—Hebrews 11:6, KJV

Are you diligently seeking Him? Do you spend more time on Facebook or Instagram than with Him?

I challenge you to keep a journal on how you spend your time and with whom you spend it for thirty days. At the end of the thirty days, revisit your journal and take note of what your pattern of time looks like and how you are spending it.

Does your life reflect God first then the rest? If not, this is an opportunity to readjust and rebalance your life and priorities. I promise if you make time for Him, you will have plenty of time to do the rest.

Be intentional. Be blessed.

# 123

When I was reading a list of abusive things a child had gone through, I remember relating to so many when I was a child. I was a child who was abused, broken, rejected, and felt unloved. I lived in an unsafe environment, and I did get taken away to foster care where I did get placed from home to home with bad and good foster parents.

But the Lord redeems and restores. It's also about perspective; I can choose to be a victim or a victor. If I hadn't walked through all of this brokenness and the Lord restored and healed me of things, I wouldn't be ready for half the assignments He gives me. For example, ministering to children, ministering out in the streets, in doctors' offices, at Walmart, any and every place you can think of. I thank God when I read this list for each and everything He walked me through. Even though it hurt, God was shaping me, molding me, and turning me into the person He needs me to be for myself and so many others. He has had a hand in my life even when I couldn't see it. I am blessed to be called His for I am His beloved, beautiful, cherished, and loved daughter.

I am reminded in Jeremiah 18:1–4 (NLT):

> This is the word that came to Jeremiah from the Lord: "Go down to the potter's house, and there I will give you my message." So I went down to the potter's house, and I saw him working at the wheel. But the pot he was shaping from the clay was marred in his hands; so the potter formed it into another pot, shaping it as seemed best to him.

Be intentional. Be blessed.

# 124

My mom has stage 4 lung cancer. There were two spots a CT scan revealed on her liver and spleen, as well as her lung. When I went to see her, we had been told there was nothing else we could do. She decided to go on hospice, but the oncologist wanted her to have another scan to see where all the cancer had spread. When I went there, the Lord asked me to pray over and anoint all the spots where the cancer was. Believing in God's power and strength, she was healed. (Praying Scary, Crazy, Amazing Prayers. This is referring to healing prayers, Scary- declaring that she is healed, healthy, and whole no matter what it looked like in the physical. Crazy-because what was in the physical compared to the spiritual, Amazing because only God could work the miracle.)

They did the scan, and guess what? Those two spots were gone in the name of Jesus! The doctors don't know how but we do. Our faith can move mountains. Healing is here. She is currently under-going radiation daily, which they said she would not be able to do either for her lung, but our God can do exceedingly and abundantly all we could ever ask for.

I give God *all* the glory, honor, and praise.

Be intentional. Be blessed.

# 125

Father, we desire to remain faithful to You all the days of our life. We join with others of the Christian faith who hold unswervingly to the hope we profess even as we spur one another on toward love and good deeds. Disappointments, seemingly unanswered prayers, loved ones who oppose us, spiritual lethargy, temptations, and trials pull at our hearts and tempt us to look back just like the Israelites who were freed from slavery. They who greatly rejoiced at their newfound freedom found themselves longing to return after the going got tough. Give us strength and firm resolve to plow through the hard soil and bumpy rocks of life all the while fixing our eyes on our eternal dwelling place as we hold unswervingly to the hope we profess in Christ Jesus, our Lord.

Be intentional. Be blessed.

# 126

A smile for the day

One of my favorite things that I find myself saying is, "That's a good spiritual nugget." So fast-forward to the other night, and this was what was said. While making cookies with my daughter, my daughter said to me, "Hey, Mom, guess what?"

"What?"

"My Holy Spirit's favorite food is spiritual nuggets."

This made me laugh out loud. She brings me so much joy!

Be intentional. Be blessed.

# 127

This week has been so awesome! God has shown me how He can shift the atmosphere and how it impacts others. At college the other day, we were to tell about ourselves including what our favorite football team was. So when it was time for me to share, and since I don't have a favorite football team but have a favorite team that I belong to, I told them boldly and confidently that I am on team Jesus and that I am involved in outreach and serving in my community. That's where my heart is fixed—on Jesus! With that being said, that evening, as I reflected, I was overwhelmed looking back on answered prayers, divine appointments, and opportunities to give back through serving.

With a humble and thankful heart, I say here I am, Lord. I will go where You want me to go and I will serve where You expect me to serve. Even if it's just for one, it's enough. And You, Lord, are more than sufficient for me.

Be intentional. Be blessed.

# 128

I am blessed beyond measure to be able to experience this week leading our niece and nephew Star and Trevor to Christ and seeing our sister Sheila this morning rededicate her life to Christ. I couldn't be more proud of them and the kingdom of heaven. To God be *all* the glory, honor, and praise!

Be intentional. Be blessed.

# 129

Praise Report

I went to register for this coming semester of college, and they gave me my dean's list certificate. Also, for those who don't know, I had met a huge milestone in my life thanks be to God. It was confirmed: I am a proud owner of an associate's degree. I am the first in my family to have a degree, and I consider it a milestone and a blessing to be able to walk in the graduation ceremony. When others thought I wouldn't amount to anything or do anything with my life, God had very different plans. Also, as an added bonus, all of the credit hours transfer directly into my bachelor's degree, which is not too far off either.

I am so excited!

Be intentional. Be blessed.

# 130

I am so thankful for the ladies the Lord has blessed and entrusted me with. In our life group Wild or Wise, I am so grateful for their hearts of faithfulness and vulnerability week after week. The Lord continues to blow me away as I humbly sit at these ladies' feet.

Be intentional. Be blessed.

# 131

Several years ago on a Wednesday night, we had to write something that the Holy Spirit had downloaded to us and give it to another sister in Christ. I didn't know then of course what I know now. The Holy Spirit had been prompting me to look through an old wallet I had before the SHE IS Brave Conference.

I will be honest with you that I was disobedient. I didn't want to look through an old wallet full of junk. Praise God for His mercy and grace. Yesterday, He prompted me again. This time I was like, "Okay, God, I'll do it." And I found a priceless treasure, a piece of paper given to me, spoken into my life by a beautiful, talented, wonderful reflection of Christ, sister Alexandra Handley. I stood there reading the words: "It's time to start living. Not time to be a chicken. Will you continue to allow God to give you doors to open and receive and slam a hand in His face? He desires to take you places in your walk with Him you'd never imagined." I could just say wow! I prayed and repented for my pure, lazy disobedience and received the message with a humble heart.

I am thankful He meets us right where we are at. Since this message was given to me years ago, I can tell you this has come true. He has taken me places I never imagined. All I had to do was let go and let God!

Lord, I'm amazed by You.

Be intentional. Be blessed.

# 132

Remember who you are serving. I am serving in the library at my daughter's school.

A random person approached me and said, "You've been in here for a long time!"

"Yes, I am serving the Lord!" I replied.

How easy is it to get wrapped up in the world? Open up your eternal eyes, ears, and mouth and recognize, amplify, lift up, and give God *all* the glory!

Any person God has placed in authority to act on His behalf whether it be your pastors, life group leaders, bosses, or anyone you are serving under recognize God has put them in that position, not man. By humbly submitting to those in authority, you are humbly submitting to God. Work as you are working for God because you are!

"Serve wholeheartedly, as if you were serving the Lord, not people" (Eph. 6:7, NIV).

Be intentional. Be blessed.

# 133

So as I anticipate and expectantly wait for today's SHE is Brave Conference, I can't help but reflect on what it has meant for me to be brave this year, not in my strength but in the Lord's strength. As I put on His armor each morning (Eph. 6:13–18, NIV), I anticipate what He might have me do each day with an excitement no one can contain!

I do not take lightly the opportunities that He has entrusted to me to impact my family, friends, and community daily. I know with my whole heart there is no greater honor in this lifetime than to do the work for His Kingdom.

I thank You, Lord, that I may open my mouth boldly to make known the mystery of the gospel, for which I am an ambassador, and that I may speak boldly as I ought to speak. "And for me, that utterance may be given unto me, that I may open my mouth boldly, to make known the mystery of the gospel, For which I am an ambassador in bonds: that therein I may speak boldly, as I ought to speak" (Eph. 6:19–20, NIV)

Be brave with your life because He paid the ultimate sacrifice.

Be intentional. Be blessed.

# 134

Father God, as I sat this morning reading Your Word and sitting with my arrow that You blessed me with through our wonderful Pastor Leisa Nelson and her staff at the SHE IS Brave Women's Conference, my heart is so full. Tears are streaming down my face, reflecting back on all the battles you have brought me through, answered prayers, and your faithfulness never to leave me nor forsake me. When others thought I was trash, You were telling me, "Oh no, you are the treasure. My daughter, you are valuable, you are loved, and I determine who you are."

You are Father God El Roi, the God Who sees.

Through my pain and longsuffering, I can gladly say I would retake it all for the one moment of being able to share a part of my testimony. Help shift the atmosphere, encourage, and proclaim Your redemptive love to the body of Christ my sisters and brothers. As I said, there is no greater honor in this lifetime than to do the work for Your kingdom.

With a humble heart, I thank you, Father.

I have had several people ask me over the past few days how I make it through a crisis. Here is the key: you keep your eyes on God, and you serve your way out of it, taking your eyes off yourself and your situation and focusing on the heart of Jesus his serving.

He tells us in Matthew 25:40 (NIV), "The King will reply, 'Truly I tell you, whatever you did for one of the least of these brothers and sisters of mine, you did for me.'"

Who are you working for, serving for, etc.? Make sure your heart is right.

Be intentional. Be blessed.

# 135

From Jessica Mathis after the SHE IS Brave Conference:

> This girl wow! Cristy Castleberry. I knew part
> of your story but never all of it. YOU ARE MY
> HERO! I have never told you this before, but you
> are one of the few that inspires me to be better
> and grow deeper in HIM. Love you bunches and
> bunches

Be intentional. Be blessed.

# 136

I pulled up to the drive through window at Zaxby's to pay for our dinner, and as I handed my card out, the lady told me that the person who was in front of me just paid for our meal and to have a blessed day. How awesome to experience God through others! Thank you to the person/persons who paid for our meal. I am very grateful!

Be intentional. Be blessed.

# 137

His Grace is sufficient.

So there was a miscommunication tonight. I had to be at the college but needed to be dropped off due to some unusual circumstances. The person who was supposed to pick me up went to one location, and I was in another. You see how this was starting to play out—not so good. So finally I called, and they explained what was communicated to them. Of course, I was not so good because I was already supposed to be there, but the Holy Spirit reminded me that I needed to be quiet and to listen. Every part of my flesh was like *Argh!*

"What would you want to be done unto you in this situation? What if it was you?"

"Well, I'd want some grace. Yes, grace. That's it."

"Okay, then give it."

So I kept my mouth shut and died to my flesh. While painful, it was so worth it. I love how He sets us up. So next, I got dropped off at the college, and unknown to me, we were not having this one make-up class that week. I called the instructor, who is super nice, because I had been out previously due to my procedure. This professor apologized and asked for grace for not letting me know that we were not having class and offered me grace in getting my class work in while out last week. Of course, I said yes. I knew at that moment; His grace is sufficient. If we extend grace freely, how much more grace will He freely give unto us? Had I not been obedient and offered my ride some grace, I would have completely missed the grace lesson, not to mention I would have dishonored God.

We have to be obedient so that He can use us. Letting go and letting God is the only way!

Be intentional. Be blessed.

# 138

Be grateful and content with what God has blessed you with because you never know when He might decide to take it away.

Be intentional. Be blessed.

# 139

I had an opportunity to support Lifeline out of Huntsville, but little did I know the Lord had a different plan for me. I attended Soul Stock, a Christian event, where there was a women's resource center booth setup. I really felt the Lord leading me to sign up to volunteer. I received the call, and I have had the honor and privilege of volunteering and serving under Amy Wright and these beautiful godly ladies. God is using the center as a vessel to help educate, heal, and restore these beautiful clients. It is a blessing to be a blessing. I have had people ask me, "Why do you volunteer in Athens when you live in Madison? It's a thirty-minute drive!" I politely smile and let them know that I am on assignment for Jesus and I go where He calls me to go. There is no greater honor in this life than to do the work for God's kingdom.

The Lord tells us in his word in 1 Peter 2:21 (NIV), "For you have been called for this purpose, since Christ suffered for you, leaving you an example for you to follow in His steps."

Last night's fantastic celebration of life with Alan and Lisa Robertson, pastors, board members, clients, client advocates, family, friends, and our community will forever resonate in my mind of God's incredible redemptive power, love, and grace.

For the speakers to be able to step out in faith and be real with us about their tests and their testimonies, to speak life into others, to give hope, and to know a God-redeemed future is what lies ahead, just waiting to be received and all we have to do is accept, isn't that Amazing?

What the devil intended to destroy us, God can turn around and employ us. We are called for an assignment, not by chance, but we are His chosen to speak out about our lives not to be silent or ashamed. Everyone you meet has a story, including yourself. Are you willing to use it for His glory?

Be intentional. Be blessed.

# 140

Sometimes, a life of faith can feel like a losing season. Sometimes, it seems like our team will never win again. The season isn't over until God says it is. Until then, we've got to stay in the game and get ready for Jesus's arrival on the scene. Stay focused. I am too blessed to be stressed.

Be intentional. Be blessed.

# 141

From Brandie Knight:

> Well thanks to a beautiful Christian woman and
> friend Cristy Castleberry, Jordan won't have to
> go back and be bullied at boys and girls club any-
> more! Thank you, God, for answering my prayer
> and delivering my baby from this awful situation!
> So blessed to have fellow sisters in Christ that
> love my baby and care about his well being!

Be intentional. Be blessed.

# 142

From Angelique:

> God was trying to use me earlier this week, but I missed it, I learned that he would not have failed me and to just be obedient even if it just seems crazy.
>
> So earlier this week I was in the hospital with Nic. And we went to the play area, there was this little boy named Mason who was in there with an injury, I had the feeling (Holy Spirit) to ask his parents can I pray for him, but I was scared and didn't know how to go about it. So I prayed to myself. But was still feeling some type of way. Well the next day my friend came to see us and we went to the play area again and lil Mason was there again, and before he and his family left the room. She stopped him and ask if they are believers and they said yes, so she asked could she pray with them and they did.
>
> Now I know when that feeling comes and keeps pushing that's the Holy Spirit. I don't want to miss out again on God using me. Obedience is better than sacrifice.
>
> Thank you Lord for using Cristy to show me that He is a Good Father.

Be intentional. Be blessed.

# 143

You hurt our witness when you are a Christian and condemn others based on their past faults and failures while knowing that you have things in the present you need to get straight yourself. Everyone is walking through something. And no, they may not be where you think they should be, but let God handle that. We are put here to build up, not tear down, and when you fail to show others compassion and kindness due to these things, don't be surprised when you get the same. Has God not extended His mercy and grace for your sins and forgiven you?

Be intentional. Be blessed.

# 144

Wow, what a night! Tea party for the T-party (treasured party). Tonight's lesson was on appearance.

She adorns herself "in respectable apparel, with modesty and self-control" (1 Tim. 2:9, ESV).

Be intentional. Be blessed.

# 145

So I want to share something. Be encouraged in the Lord. I have been going to college full-time to finish my business degree. My Business Law class was a setup for a God encounter. There were nights when I would leave the class wondering what in the world I got myself into. It felt like it was a moving target. I just couldn't catch. I was like, God you led me to go back to school. I would constantly not know where I stood in the class with grades and everything. I would write my research paper only to have it marked out in front of me, literally—not one, not two, but three times or more. Did this feel good? No. In my frustration, I would plead with God through prayer and the word. "But you said I could do this. You say, 'I can do all things through You who strengthens me,' (Phil. 4:13, NKJV) and I claim that and stand on it. What am I missing? What are you trying to teach me?" Then the answer came.

"But, Cristy, how many times have I been rejected?"

"Hmmm… okay, God. I get what You are saying to me now." It wasn't until I got the part about rejection—His lesson for me—that I received a perfect mark on my research paper. How many times do we quit when getting frustrated because we are rejected? And how many are willing to stay on a promise God has given to us and stay it through even when rejected over and over? God is always faithful and always on time.

"'For I know the plans I have for you,' declares the Lord, 'plans to prosper you and not to harm you, plans to give you hope and a future'" (Jer. 29:11, NIV).

Be intentional. Be blessed.

# 146

Making a difference may not lead to greatness.

Perhaps you will seem to do little more than being a faithful friend, girlfriend or boyfriend, spouse, caring parent, or growing disciple of Jesus, but these are the things from which God makes a difference in other people's lives. In God's hands, little differences become big.

Be intentional. Be blessed.

# 147

The power of God's Word and Spirit is the key to overcoming anger. Pray.

After having stripped away our anger, then we can finally put on love and self-control. Without stripping out the source, i.e. the actual cause for anger, it is much like putting a fresh layer of paint on a dirty wall—it would peel off in no time.

First, peel off the source, and then you can lay the paint right on the wall and it will stick.

Afterward, healing can occur, and you will be surprised at how the light will reflect in and on that fresh coat of paint. God makes all things beautiful in his time.

Be intentional. Be blessed.

# 148

Deal with your anger (James 1:19–20).

Unresolved anger is always evil. We must not become complacent to it. We must understand that our anger will not achieve God's mission.

"[This] you know, my beloved brethren. But let everyone be quick to hear, slow to speak [and] slow to anger for the anger of man does not achieve the righteousness of God" (James 1:19–20, NASB).

Try to remember that apologizing does not mean that the other party did no wrong. They may not apologize, but it is our responsibility to move forward and straighten out our relationships with others.

Be intentional. Be blessed.

# 149

Die to self; live by Christ (Gal. 2:20, NIV).

I have died to myself; I now live for Christ.

We make a choice to walk not as a victim but as a victor! Consciously allowing Christ to live out His life in us is a necessary part of deliverance from anger and cannot be done apart from Him. When you choose this, you open yourself to Christ's inner healing.

There are two aspects to dying to self: There is the old made new where you dedicate your new life to starting over and doing what is right. Then there is also a daily dying to self or your flesh so that your spirit may grow day by day reading the word and by daily morning prayer where you submit your day and life to the Lord.

"I have been crucified with Christ, and it is no longer I who live, but Christ lives in me; and the life which I now live in the flesh I live by faith in the Son of God, who loved me, and delivered Himself up for me" (Gal. 2:20, NIV).

Be intentional. Be blessed.

# 150

Break the stronghold of anger (2 Cor. 10:3–7).

May God abolish every last lie that so easily ensnares us!

A stronghold is a concealed sin that we have given up hope on ever being victorious over. See, I have tried to overcome this anger in the past, and I just can't seem to cut it out. I feel like a loser, and I am disheartened by it so there has to be some final cover-up for it.

Truth, however, gives confidence and ability to do what is right even if no one is looking. Our character is personally who we are when no one else is looking but God, and unless God intervenes, we will only pretend to be an overcomer and the lies will block out the light and strip every ounce of confidence that was left in us ever overcoming this problem.

From the verses given to us in the Bible urging us to deal compassionately with people rather than in anger or rage, it is apparent that we are responsible and more than capable through Christ to overcome this hold of wrath.

Some of the common lies that cause us to minimize the problem of anger and therefore prevent us from overcoming violence are the following:

"He or she had it coming."
"I was so upset by him or her. I need to get revenge."
"I can't help it. It's just the way I am."
"I was born that way."
"My parents passed this down."
"It's not as bad as it seems."
"My anger is getting better. I promise."

Hope and healing come when we are truly broken before God and have a godly sorrow over our sin. We welcome Him to overcome the sin in our lives. Realizing that without Him there is no way to overcome it, we have to repent with a right heart and motive. More often than not, our pride minimizes our anger's wrongs and makes exceptions and excuses for our bad behaviors.

Here are a few scriptures to help combat this stronghold.

> For though we walk in the flesh, we do not war according to the flesh, for the weapons of our warfare are not of the flesh, but divinely powerful for the destruction of fortresses. We are destroying speculations, and every lofty thing raised up against the knowledge of God, and we are taking every thought captive to the obedience of Christ. (2 Cor. 10:3-5, NASB)

> He who is slow to anger has great understanding, But he who is quick-tempered exalts folly. (Prov. 14:29, NASB).

> Love is patient, love is kind, and is not jealous; love does not brag and is not arrogant, does not act unbecomingly; it does not seek its own, is not provoked, does not take into account a wrong suffered. (1 Cor. 13:4–5, NASB)

> I can do all things through Christ, who strengthens me. (Phil. 4:13, NKJV)

Be intentional. Be blessed.

# 151

Replace anger with acts of kindness (Eph. 4:31).

Anger must be uprooted but replaced with fruits of the Spirit.

Replacing our fiery spirit with a loving spirit is something only the Lord can do. Our primary focus has to be on what we should do and not on what we shouldn't do. The Lord tells us in His word to be transformed. By what? The renewing of our mind. To renew the mind requires focusing on godly thoughts and actions. What would Jesus be doing if He were on the scene? Write down things you can do to bring about healing, sincerely apologizing, restitution, whatever the Lord lays in your heart to do. An example is breaking property. You can offer to pay for and replace the item. The Lord is obvious in what we should and should not be doing, so let us put away the following:

"Let all bitterness and wrath and anger and clamor and slander be put away from you, along with malice. And be kind to one another, tender-hearted, forgiving each other, just as God in Christ also has forgiven you" (Ephesians 4:31–32, NASB).

Be intentional. Be blessed.

# 152

Fully deal with each day's anger (Eph. 4:26).

Make sure before we turn in, we deal with our anger.

Scripture tells us to resolve our anger before the sun goes down, and there is a significant reason for that because unresolved anger escalates into wrath.

Have you made commitments before going to bed to resolve the anger in your home? This can be with your spouse, grandparents, and extended family.

As a parent, regardless of your exhaustion, anger is not an excuse, and you have to commit yourself to make peace with your children before they sleep as well.

"Be angry and do not sin. Don't let the sun go down on your anger" (Eph. 4:26, CSB).

Be intentional. Be blessed.

# 153

In closing to the steps of overcoming anger, I would like to close with the following thoughts:

What we do with anger will affect our lives in many ways. It will also make a difference in others' lives too. As God pointed out to Cain, anger is like a huge billboard in our path which warns: What you do next matters!

Anger is a reaction looking for a way to express itself. Anger does not think. That's why we have to think for it when we get angry. Without a master, anger hurts and destroys. Mastered, anger offers a forceful response to wrong. If we have a problem with anger, we need to listen carefully to God's warning to Cain. Letting God master our anger will make a difference to you and others.

God Bless you ALL and thank you for allowing me to share God's amazing Word with you.

Be intentional. Be blessed.

# 154

This sweet girl, my daughter, who has such a heart to serve her community, has been asking me for a very long time if she can go to a nursing home type of place and love the residents. "This is my dream, mama."

Well today, through Huntsville Dream Center Outreach, her dream came true.

I cannot express how much this truly meant to her. She could have been sleeping in, playing her DS, etc., but she chose to serve in our community today. Loving, laughing, living, and sharing Jesus Christ.

I am proud of the young lady she is becoming.

Be intentional. Be blessed.

# 155

While I'm Waiting
By: John Waller

I'm waiting
I'm waiting on You, Lord
And I am hopeful
I'm waiting on You, Lord
Though it is painful
But patiently, I will wait
I will move ahead, bold and confident
Taking every step in obedience

While I'm waiting
I will serve You
While I'm Waiting
I will not faint
I'll be running the race
Even while I wait

I'm waiting
I'm waiting on You, Lord
And I am peaceful
I'm waiting on You, Lord
Though it's not easy
But faithfully, I will wait
Yes, I will wait…

Be intentional. Be blessed.

# 156

I am reminded how much our faith gets stretched when we are down to our last. I was down to my final three miles, and I could have been stricken with panic and fear that I would run out of gas. I was already on my way on the highway as I heard the ding of the car letting me know I needed to get gas. I said, "Okay, God, I am trusting You. I don't know how many miles to the gas station, but I am trusting You that You do and that You will get me there."

How many times are we down to our last mile, dime, hope, and God is like, "Trust Me, I got you." Will you trust?

"Now faith is the substance of things hoped for, the evidence of things not seen" (Heb. 11:1, KJV).

Have faith and see what God can do for you.

I am walking by faith.

Be intentional. Be blessed.

# 157

So blessed, I went to a place to get ice cream today with my daughter, and after having a pleasant conversation with the lady, she gave me a 15 percent discount at the register. I was not expecting anything. I immediately thanked her for being a blessing to me today and thanked God for His provision.

He is a good father, and He loves me.

Be intentional. Be blessed.

# 158

While I was completely wrecked, God's divine appointments are incredible.

If only people really knew the power of prayer. I got the opportunity for God to use me to pray for healing over a woman who sat beside me during the previewing of the movie *War Room* (a must see). She had a tumor removed, but when she showed me her leg, it didn't look right. It looked like the infection was spreading. I praise God and give Him all the glory, honor, and praise.

Thank you, Jesus.

Be intentional. Be blessed.

# 159

First, I want to thank you, God, for it is only in Your strength that I was able to complete this school. Next, I would like to thank all of the people who wrote references for me both pastoral and friend. Thank you to the staff and leadership of the Elijah House School of Prayer Ministry and my church family. Thank you to all my family and friends who have supported me and believed in me.

No words can truly express my gratitude to all of the individuals who have poured into my life during this season.

I am overwhelmed by God's goodness.

Be intentional. Be blessed.

# 160

So thankful for divine appointments. I had to go to Walmart money center to take care of a bill, and the lady at the counter saved me some money. I said out loud, "Praise God. You are my blessing!" I said thank you.

She said, "You are quite welcome." Then that nudge came. I asked her if there was anything I could pray for her about. My heart was racing. If I didn't ask her now, I would miss the opportunity entirely. "Okay, God. I trust You more than how crazy I am about to look." So I asked her if there was anything she needed prayer about that I could pray for her specifically for. She said, "Actually, yes. Please pray for peace for me in the workplace and for the return of my furniture." I said it would be my pleasure and immediately started praying for her. She was so thankful.

You never know what someone is battling, and how god is going to use you or your resources on hand so that His Kingdom can be impacted.

Following up, this lady had her furniture restored to her, and her prayer was answered.

Be intentional. Be blessed.

# 161

Spiritual discernment—pay attention to it because it will assist you to make a good decision when things are not quite right.

Be intentional. Be blessed.

# 162

Truth: It may not lead you to where you thought you were going, but it will always lead you somewhere better. When ignored, it will eventually show itself. The intimacy of your relationships is directly proportional to the degree to which you have revealed the truth about yourself.

Be intentional. Be blessed.

# 163

Having your conduct honorable among the Gentiles, that. They may, by your good works which thy observe, glorify God.

—1 Peter 2:12

The Apostle Peter said, "This is the will of God, that by doing good you may put to silence the ignorance of foolish men" (1 Pet. 2:15, NKJV)

> I like the following:
> Lord, may our words and deeds be true,
> As people of the light,
> And help us as we follow You
> To always do what's right.

—Charles H. Spurgeon

There are no degrees of honesty.
Be intentional. Be blessed.

# 164

When someone else gets favor, don't be a hater; just be a congratulator! Trust in God. Yours will come.

Be intentional. Be blessed.

# 165

No one can steal your joy unless you let them.
Be intentional. Be blessed.

# 166

He uses even our greatest error and deepest pain to mold us into a better person.

Be intentional. Be blessed.

# 167

"Submit yourselves therefore to God. Resist the devil, and he will flee from you" (James 4:7, ESV).

Be intentional. Be blessed.

# 168

Whoever pursues righteousness and love finds life, prosperity [a] and honor.

—Proverbs 21:21, NKJV

We should always be in the pursuit of God because He is righteousness and love. If you seek Him with all of your mind, heart, and soul, He can be found. We are never alone.

Be intentional. Be blessed.

# 169

What consumes your mind controls your life.
Be intentional. Be blessed.

# 170

"Aspire to inspire before you expire," said Robert Rohm. Be intentional. Be blessed.

# 171

Jesus said, "The Spirit of the Lord (is) upon Me, because He has anointed Me (the anointed one, the Messiah) to preach the good news of (the Gospel) to the poor; He has sent me to announce release to the captives and recovery of sight to the blind, to send forth as delivered those who are oppressed (who are downtrodden, bruised, crushed, and broken down by calamity), to proclaim the accepted and acceptable year of the Lord (the day when salvation and the free favors of God profusely abound)" ( Luke 4:18–19, NLT).

Enough said!

Be intentional. Be blessed.

# 172

And after you have suffered a little while, the God of all grace [Who imparts all blessing and favor], Who has called you to His [Own] eternal glory in Christ Jesus, will Himself complete and make you what you ought to be, establish and ground you securely, and strengthen, and settle you.

—1 Peter 5:10, AMP

Suffering is no fun for any one of us, but we will all go through it at some point. Some have harder assignments than others, but suffering is still suffering. These tests are our testimony to reach others.

When people watch as we turn to God for help in our hardships, they see our victories. It provides a witness to them. In many times, we walked through life thinking no one is watching. However, there is always someone watching. We should live our lives in such a manner that we are a true reflection of Christ. We should be so full of Christ that others will be drawn to Him. Notice that I said drawn to Him, not us (our fleshy person).

Praise Him in the midst of your storms and happy times and watch what He can do. He will never leave you nor forsake you even though you may be walking through the valley of the shadow of death. You don't have to fear because He is with you, He goes before you, and He sees you.

Be intentional. Be blessed.

# 173

The weapons we fight with are not the weapons of the world. On the contrary, they have divine power to demolish strongholds. We demolish arguments and every pretension that sets itself up against the knowledge of God, and we take captive every thought to make it obedient to Christ.

—2 Corinthians 10:4–5, NIV

Satan usually doesn't overwhelm us with powerful desires. Instead, he starts with the little things: little dissatisfactions, small desires, and it builds from there. That's how Satan works: slowly, diligently, and in small ways, all he needs is an opening. We have to be aware of Satan's deceptive ways. It's always the appeal of sin or Satanic enticement. The temptation is not to do evil or to cause harm or bring injustice. The lure is that we will gain something.

I praise God that we can have victory over Satan's schemes through knowledge of our Lord and Savior Jesus Christ.

Be intentional. Be blessed.

# 174

Therefore, [there is] now no condemnation (no adjudging guilty of wrong) for those who are in Christ Jesus, who live [and] walk not after the dictates of the flesh, but after the dictates of the spirit.

—Romans 8:1, AMPC

Have you ever felt like or known that you completely blew it? I have. God gave me a test, and I failed. Well, what happens after that? The moment you fail is an open doorway for Satan to waltz right in and take over your thoughts with lies: You will never be worthy. He can't use you, you are too far gone now. And so on.

His goal is to keep you feeling so condemned that you won't want to get back up again. Satan knows that once you choose right thoughts and actions and reject the wrong ones, his control is over. The Word says, "Therefore if anyone is in Christ, he is a new creation. The old has passed away; behold, the new has come" (2 Cor. 5:17, ESV).

All power and authority have been given to us through Christ Jesus. Therefore, we can do all things through Christ who strengthens us. Recognize you have the authority and power to rebuke Satan and put him in his place.

Be intentional. Be blessed.

# 175

All of us trip, fall, and scrape our knees, but when we're encouraged, we get back up and try again. We misjudge Satan's persistence. He will continue to try and can trip you up if you are not on alert or prepared for his same old schemes. His goal is to make you feel so worthless which is condemnation that you won't want to get up again. "If God is for us, who can be against us?" (Rom. 8:31, NIV).

Be intentional. Be blessed.

# 176

What I have forgiven has been for your sakes to keep Satan from getting the advantage over us; for we are not ignorant of his wiles and intentions.

—2 Cor. 2:10–11, AMPC

Satan attacks you in your mind so you will act out in your flesh.

Today, Satan tried to attack me while eating brunch with my family. It starts with a thought. He decided to use something from my past years ago, but I was completely aware of what was going on. So I prayed while at the table. He was trying to get me to act out of my flesh, but I rebuked it in the name of Jesus!

I am a new creation in Christ, and I can do all things through Christ who strengthens me. Years ago, I would have acted out of my flesh, and Satan would have had a party because of the chaos and confusion It would have caused my family to be divided and hurt emotionally because of the lies that Satan was trying to feed me to destroy me. I am proud to say that because of my relationship with Jesus Christ, I am an overcomer and conqueror through Him.

"You, dear children, are from God and have overcome them, because the one who is in you is greater than the one who is in the world" (1 John 4:4, NIV).

Thank you, God, for not leaving me where you found me years ago.

Be intentional. Be blessed.

# 177

God has been telling me of how precious life is all day long as I have been spending time with my sisters, nieces, nephews, and my mother. The smiles on their faces, their warm embraces, and their laughter; these are the moments that I will cherish all my life.

"The best and most beautiful things in the world cannot be seen or even touched—they must be felt with the heart," said Helen Keller.

Be intentional. Be blessed.

# 178

A season of suffering is a small assignment when compared to the reward.

Rather than begrudge your problem, explore it, ponder it, and most of all, use it. Use it to the glory of God.

Be intentional. Be blessed.

# 179

Discouragement destroys hope. Failure quickly leads to more failure. And once we allow our minds to say, "This is the way it will always be," the evil one has won a victory over us. We can say to ourselves, "Lord Jesus, with Your help, I can make it. With Your help, I won't be discouraged and feel hopeless. With Your help, I can defeat every wrong thought the devil slips into my mind. Thank you for victory over my life."

Be intentional. Be blessed.

# 180

Jesus said, go; it shall be done for you as you have believed.

—Matthew 8:13, NIV

Thank You, God, for every deliverance in my life. Thank You for setting me free from negative and wrong thinking. Thank You for defeating Satan in this area of my life.

Be intentional. Be blessed.

# 181

We are assured and know that [God being a partner in their labor] all things work together and are [fitting into a plan] for good to and for those who love God and are called according to [His] design and purpose.

—Romans 8:28, AMPC

Do not lose heart. Continuing to trust God is the key to victory in painful and seemingly unjust situations. Faith and prayer move the hand of God if we keep believing. He promises to continue moving on our behalf to work everything out for good.

Be intentional. Be blessed.

# 182

"You are from God, little children, and have overcome them; because greater is He who is in you than he who is in the world" (1 John 4:4, NASB).

Be intentional. Be blessed.

# 183

Satan first attacks us in our minds. He knows if he can get us to think to ourselves or through someone else that we are bad or absolute failures and can get us to condemn ourselves, then he has won. He now has our thoughts and feelings under his control and can cause us and use us to overreact and not conduct ourselves the way God would want us to. God says there is no condemnation; we can control our minds and control our feelings and live a positive life free from Satan. Satan, I rebuke you in the name of Jesus and am very aware of what you are trying to do. Amen

Be intentional. Be blessed.

# 184

"Lean on, trust in, and be confident in the Lord with all your heart and mind and do not rely on your own insight or understanding. In all your ways know, recognize, and acknowledge Him, and He will direct and make straight and plain your paths." (Proverbs 3:5–6, AMPC)

Be intentional. Be blessed.

# 185

Therefore, if any person is [engrafted] in Christ (the Messiah) he is a new creation (a new creature altogether); the old [previous moral and spiritual condition] has passed away. Behold, the fresh and new has come!

—2 Cor. 5:17, AMPC

Be filled with joy and think positive, loving thoughts so that Satan has no stronghold over your mind.

Be intentional. Be blessed.

# 186

Evaluate your shortcomings and failures instead of focusing on other people and what you think is wrong with them. When we tend to look at others, the illusion is that our stuff will be easier and less painful. As long as you can keep the focus on other individuals, then you don't have to examine your heart.

Lord, please renew my spirit and continue to make in me a loving and upright heart.

Be intentional. Be blessed.

# 187

Dear Father in heaven, forgive my unbelief at times. Excuse me for allowing Satan to deceive me or for letting him help me to think I'm worthless or unworthy of Your amazing miracles. I am worthy because You have made me worthy. I am a daughter or a son of the highest. You are the God of the impossible, and I ask You to help me wait on You and never give up so that the possible can happen. Forgive me please when I have gotten ahead of Your divine plan. Help me to wait well. Thank You that Your love never returns void, and it never runs out on me.

Be intentional. Be blessed.

# 188

Blessings are not a result of anything to do with us. They are the result of God being evident in our lives.

Check out Isaiah 30:18 (AMPC).

Loving God, thank You, for your unmerited favor. Even though the evil one tries to make me feel unfit, please remind me that I am a child, Your child, and You are my loving Father. My relationship to You makes me deserving, and I thank You for that. Amen.

Be intentional. Be blessed.

# 189

Two years ago, God caused a significant event in my life to happen to help shape and mold me into something better. At the time, it was challenging and painful, but I am forever grateful. We can be victorious and can overcome anything with God's help!

Glory be to God today and always!

Be intentional. Be blessed.

# 190

Dear Lord Jesus, through so many days in my life, I have been robbed of my joy and contentment by evil forebodings. As those feelings come to me, please remind me that You are in control. Help me to rest in You and rejoice in Your power in my life.

Be intentional. Be blessed.

# 191

I am really enjoying my life! It's so great to live, laugh, love, and be happy even when the storms of life are raging. Praise God! He is good *all* the time!

Be intentional. Be blessed.

# 192

I had a great time at the stepfamily seminar tonight. I am looking forward to what God has in store for me. I am prepared and willing to receive my blessings from Him whether it be a wonderful husband or a life of singleness.

I am content with God's plan for my life.

Be intentional. Be blessed.

# 193

Consider it wholly joyful, my brethren, whenever you are enveloped in or encounter trials of any sort or fall into various temptations. Be assured and understand that the trial and proving of your faith bring out endurance and steadfastness and patience. But let endurance and steadfastness and patience have full play and do a thorough work so that you may be [people] perfectly and fully developed [With no defects], lacking in nothing.

—James 1:2–4, AMPC

Holy Spirit of God, help me always to believe Your promises even when I don't understand Your purpose. I want to learn to trust You more as I move forward in faith to accomplish what You have for me to do. Help me always to be obedient.

Be intentional. Be blessed.

# 194

I had wonderful fellowship with my friend Susan Abernathy today. Even though she didn't know me very well at the time when I was going through a lot medically with surgeries, she was the only one who came to visit me besides my friend's family. She brought me some homemade soup, *Shattered Magazine*, and some DVDs to watch or listen to. I got a chance to tell her how much she touched my life today by her acts of kindness. God knew exactly what I needed. He is always faithful and loving. I am so thankful for her.

Be intentional. Be blessed.

# 195

Sitting down, Jesus called the Twelve and said, "Anyone who wants to be first must be the very last, and the servant of all."

—Mark 9:35, NIV

I am reminded of how we are to sit at the feet of others and humbly serve one another by learning from, teaching, serving, loving, and growing together in Christ. How many times do we struggle with giving time, money, etc.? How many awesome opportunities do we have to serve God's people yet give into selfishness? I have learned from experience that even though I may be going through the valley of the shadow of death, if I take my eyes off myself and serve others, how quickly God can turn my situation around and what the devil intended for harm can be used for His Glory.

Be intentional. Be blessed.

# 196

Ever had someone jump to conclusions about what is going on in your life? Or maybe they heard just a part of your conversation and ran off to tell everyone, missing what was truly said and then gossiping about it and making false accusations.

I know I have experienced this against me, and it's very hard in the flesh to not want to do something about it while God is like, "I got this. Chill out."

If I keep silent and listen to God's prompting instead of taking matters into my own hands, He will make things right. He goes before me. He already knows what situation or event I am about to face. The key is to trust Him. He works all things together for the good of those who love Him.

In the end, those people will be silenced and exposed, revealing the truth.

Remember: before taking matters into your own hands, take it to God.

"It is God's will that your honorable lives should silence those ignorant people who make foolish accusations against you" (1 Pet. 2:15, NLT).

Be intentional. Be blessed.

# 197

I just want to take a moment to thank God for entrusting me to pour into the lives of others. There is no greater honor than to do the work for God's kingdom. To Him be *all* the glory, honor, and praise.

Be intentional. Be blessed.

# 198

Food for thought: Are you and your husband or wife having break-fast and dinner together? The food that you receive provides nourish-ment to your body throughout your day. I am not just talking about earthly food but spiritual food. Are you reading the word or holding a devotional together and praying together? You would be amazed at how God can transform you and your marriage while setting the mood for your day if you take the time to put Him first as a couple, soaking up God's Word and His amazing love together. It's one of the most intimate encounters we can have with God and each other.

"Therefore, what God has joined together, let no one separate" (Mark 10:9, NIV).

Be intentional. Be blessed.

# 199

So on Sunday, I missed an opportunity to pray for a sister in Christ. I ask her how she was doing and she said, "I have been sick for a while, but I am recovering." I knew then that I should have prayed for healing over her sick body, but I didn't listen to the nudge from God. This resulted in a missed opportunity. I asked God to forgive me for my disobedience after that happened. On Wednesday night, I had someone directly come up to me and ask for me to pray for healing for her granddaughter. I was so honored I could have shouted to the top of my lungs: "Thank You, Jesus!" Praise the Lord! I know it is only through Him that I received that opportunity to lay my hands on her sick body and pray for her. I give God *all* the honor and glory. I am completely humbled.

I love how He redeems.

Be intentional. Be blessed.

# 200

Do not be deceived: God cannot be mocked. A man reaps what he sows. Whoever sows to please their flesh, from the flesh will reap destruction; whoever sows to please the Spirit, from the Spirit will reap eternal life.

—Galatians 6:7–8, NIV

Father God, please help me to quickly discern your assignments for me and to respond to the Holy Spirit's promptings. Often, You speak to me through words, more specifically the Word: scriptures, daily prayers, and worship. You also talk to me through the undesirable consequences that come from acts of disobedience through my fleshly ways. Help me to see Your warning—caution lights and stop lights—to keep me from the dangerous toils and snares of the evil one. Thank You for redirecting me even when I felt that it was an inconvenience to me. That disadvantage turned out to be a blessing in disguise. Help me to sow good seeds. I want more of You and less of me. I want eternal life through You, my Lord and Savior.

Be intentional. Be blessed.

# 201

God gives us great opportunities if we only listen. After the Champions Summit Leadership Conference, I was hungry. I decided to go to Taco Bell. As I passed by Taco Bell, I said to myself, *I wanted Taco Bell. Why did I pass it?* Then I was like, *Okay, I will go to a different fast-food place then.* I passed it again. Again, I said the same thing, so I was like, *Um… okay, I will turn around and go back.* And as I drove, I still felt like I was in a state of confusion about where I should be going. So I said, "Okay, God, take me where You want." So I had no clue where I was going. Finally, I ended up at Cheddars. I said, "What do you expect me to do here?"

I went in, and right as they said, "How many?" I immediately said, "It's just me, and I don't want to sit at the bar." They immediately told me they had a table for me. I thought that was rather strange because there were tons of other people waiting for buzzers, and they could have seated at least four at the table they are seating me at.

My waitress came to the table, and I asked, "How are you doing?"

She said, "I am good."

And I immediately responded, "Okay, let's be for real."

I could discern that something was wrong, and she looked at me and said, "You know, I could really use a hug today." I got up from my seat and hugged her. People were staring at me and all. She needed to know someone cares about here and loves her. She needed the love of Christ. I felt that subtle nudge. So I left the name and address of our church. I am so thankful He calls even the unqualified—myself—to be used for His glory.

Thank you, God, for using me.

Be intentional. Be blessed.

# 202

Difficult times will come. Hang in there with God and watch what He will do!

"Yes, I have loved you with an everlasting love; Therefore with lovingkindness, I have drawn you. Again I will build you, and you shall be rebuilt" (Jer. 31:34, NKJV).

Be intentional. Be blessed.

# 203

Are you encouraging your boyfriend or husband to be a leader in your relationship or family?

When he steps out in faith and takes the risk, please affirm him. You might be pretty surprised with what kind of response you will receive.

Build him up. "Fathers can give their sons an inheritance of houses and wealth, but only the Lord can give an understanding wife" (Prov. 19:14, NLT).

Be intentional. Be blessed.

# 204

As trials keep being thrown at me, I am reminded of this: "But in that coming day no weapon turned against you will succeed. You will silence every voice raised up to accuse you. These benefits are enjoyed by the servants of the LORD; their vindication will come from me. I the LORD, have spoken!" (Isa. 54:17, NLT).

Be intentional. Be blessed.

# 205

Just saw *Annie* with my daughter Latiara. Best movie I have seen in a long time! If you have ever been in foster care like I have, you can definitely relate! Tears were flowing. I loved it!

I am not ashamed of where I come from or where I have been. You don't have to be either.

Be intentional. Be blessed.

# 206

As I was walking out of Walmart, God gave me an opportunity to bless an elderly lady. I was walking rather quickly behind her so I could get the door for her when she stopped, and I almost ran into her. She said, "I am so sorry."

I said, "No, ma'am. I was in a rush to get the door for you." I wish you could have seen her face brighten up with a huge smile as I patiently waited for her at the door.

When she went to the door, she said, "Thank you so much, and you have a Merry Christmas."

I told her, "Thank you and God bless."

I am reminded that it's the little opportunities we often miss due to being in a rush. How many more opportunities would he give us if we listened and waited with expectancy?

Praise God from Whom all blessings flow.

Be intentional. Be blessed.

# 207

It's the little glimpses of God that continue to blow my mind. Maybe it can bring someone hope or encouragement on God's faithfulness.

I was standing in my bathroom a couple of days ago unpacking my makeup, and I had thought that I needed more Mary Kay foundation. Yesterday, I won the Mary Kay gift certificate at the SHE Moms Christmas party. I know it's a God thing because He is the only one Who knew I needed more Mary Kay foundation.

I praise God and thank Him for his love, mercy, and grace. This is not the first time He has done this. When I needed *The Holy Spirit: An Introduction* by John Bevere for our life group, He led me to attend the Next Steps 201 class to join the church. Reluctantly, I listened and went, and they gave away the book. God is always faithful and always on time. Even if he doesn't give me what I want, He always provides everything I need.

Be intentional. Be blessed.

# 208

Have you ever judged someone based on their looks, attitudes, or how they act? Have you ever judged someone else's motives before asking?

I am reminded this morning during the reading of this message. "But, O Lord of hosts, You who test the righteous, and see the mind and heart" (Jer. 20:12, NKJV).

Only The Lord can see someone's mind and heart, and a lot of times we have no clue what is going on with them. We only see the surface and say, "Well, they must be this or that," based on what we see outwardly.

We should be careful of passing judgment on others when we do the same things.

Be intentional. Be blessed.

# 209

Today is a great day to give thanks to the Lord, as is every day, and to serve others. I am reminded of Mary sitting at Jesus's feet humbly serving Him. He saw more than just the act of what she was doing; He saw her heart. As we press on today with thanksgiving, it reminds me that we are to sit at the feet of others and to see their hearts. There is more to a person than just their surface. You never know what battle they are facing on the inside. Though they may be knocked down, He can use you to help them back up again. He doesn't wait around for you to get qualified by the worldly standards; He will use you right where you are at.

"You, dear children, are from God and have overcome them, because the one who is in you is greater than the one who is in the world" (1 John 4:4, NIV).

Happy Thanksgiving!

Be intentional. Be blessed.

# 210

I had the incredible privilege of having great fellowship and food with some exceptional ladies today: Susan, Joy, Robin, Lisa, Johnnie, and Shirley. The décor was beautiful too! It meant a lot to me that there was a special place marked for each one of us. It reminded me of how God sees us and how He has a special place for all of us at His table.

Be intentional. Be blessed.

# 211

Do you pray with your child or children before they go to school? Do you know what he or she or they are packing to school? I know what my child is packing, and though she may not be packing lunch to school every day, you can bet she is packing a lesson from God to share with everyone at the lunch table.

Be intentional. Be blessed.

# 212

If you ever want to know how much you have changed, browse the contents of your iPod you listened to years ago. Thank God I am not who I use to be! I am striving daily to be a better person and to bring glory to His kingdom.

Be intentional. Be blessed.

# 213

Do you ever greet someone with a good morning, good afternoon, or good evening as you are going through the drive thru? A lot of times, we are so stuck on being in a rush that we forget that the people at the window are serving us. Yes, I said it, serving us. Underappreciated, they are human beings too. Just as no one wants to be treated as less than another, take the time to reach out and ask how their day is going and watch their face light up. Say thank you. All of these things can go a long way.

"Let His light shine in this darkened world. Greater is He that is in you than He that is in the world" (1 John 4:4, KJV).

Be intentional. Be blessed.

# 214

God is always faithful and always on time.

Have you ever had to step out of your comfort zone into the unknown because you felt that nudge from God?

You know where He is telling you to go, but you don't exactly know why until you arrive at your destination. Sometimes, it may be just a test of obedience. This happened to me yesterday. He placed me at a location not just for obedience but to show me something, my people. He said, "Go and preach the Gospel to my people, not just my children, Christians, but my people, those who are in need of a Savior." As I looked out, I could see exactly why God had placed me there. He used part of my test/testimony of my past to allow me to minister the Gospel of Jesus Christ to these individuals by introducing myself. I was allowed to plant a God seed. When we love, we love the least of us.

I am so moved by His divine encounters.

Be intentional. Be blessed.

# 215

Leaving a life and a legacy of love, I once met a man named Marshall Gurley, who impacted lives like no other, being a pastor for many churches, a mentor, and a friend. If you were around him, you knew you were in the presence of the Lord. I challenge us all to really actually think about the legacy we are sowing right now and the legacy we will leave when we leave this earth. I know that when Marshall got to Heaven, God could definitely say, "Very good, my loyal and faithful servant." This is my prayer: to live a life and to leave a legacy that is pleasing and honoring to God.

Be intentional. Be blessed.

# 216

For this is the message you heard from the beginning: We should love one another.

—1 John 3:11, NIV

Take a moment to reflect on what this truly means. Should we love one another only when the circumstances seem right? When we will get something in return? No. We should love one another at all times. Remember when you do this, regardless of whether you can see the bigger picture, you are planting seeds that will affect generations to come.

Be intentional. Be blessed.

# 217

I was going to take some stuff to Asbury Thrift Store today because I was combining and downsizing due to having extra items that I don't need. I needed to get Latiara's medicine and but completely forgot to take the stuff with me. I got to the pharmacy, and the lady told me that it was not filled and she was not sure why I received a text saying that it was.

So, she said, "I will go ahead and put it in to be filled and come back in about twenty minutes."

I said, "Okay, no problem." So the thrift store is five minutes down the road five minutes, so I decided to go over there to kill some time. I was walking around, and all of a sudden, I found myself in a place where I couldn't go around the people standing in the aisle. A lady walked up to them and started talking to them, and in my head, I was like, *Don't be nosey and don't listen.* and I will just say excuse me to them and keep moving; all the while, my discernment was telling me to listen.

I turned my back trying to not be all up in their conversation. I heard a woman telling another that her husband passed away and she has three children, but they lost everything. Someone had been kind enough to donate a house to them, but they have nothing to fill it with. I knew at that very moment why I couldn't get through the aisle.

I took a step of faith and allowed God to use me. I said, "Excuse me. I couldn't help hearing your conversation, and it just so happens that I have things that I am going through right now. We have extra items that we were going to get rid of. Would you like to have them?" They were shocked. I asked for their names and numbers.

I could see the tears welling up in their eyes. She said, "I don't have the money to pay for it."

"I said, "Don't worry. It's paid in full. God bless you."

When you say, "Here I am, Lord. Use me," be ready for the most amazing ride of your life! There is no greater honor than to do the work for His Kingdom."

Be intentional. Be blessed

# 218

So I was sitting in the social security office; and right away as I checked in, I could just feel this very down, depressed, drab, silent state in the room. So the more I sat there, a thought popped in my mind, *When they call my number, I am going to yell 'Bingo!' and liven this place up a bit.* You know, provide some happiness to this location. An hour goes by, then all of a sudden, my number gets called, and I yell out "Bingo!" I wish everyone could have seen the people laughing and smiling at that point in the room.

Thank You, Jesus, for using me to bring happiness to a roomful of strangers who needed to see you.

To God be *all* the Glory!!!

Be intentional. Be blessed.

# 219

Redemptive hope, what is it?
What God can do for another, he can do for you.
Be intentional. Be blessed.

# 220

A changing world needs the Word of God to stabilize it. I, living in a fluctuating world, need the Word of God to sustain me.

Be intentional. Be blessed.

# 221

Even though my daughter and I were both really sick the other day and both at the doctor's office, upon checkout, she said, "Momma, I would like to donate to this!" She took the time to donate her own money to a great cause. And yes, I stress that it is her own money! No prompting, bribing, etc.

Thank You, Jesus, for this moment with her. Over the years with her, I have seen her heart grow more and more in love with God. I am so thankful that God is using her as a young child to impact His kingdom.

It makes this momma proud!

Be intentional. Be blessed.

# 222

This makes me think about what I tell Latiara every morning before she goes to school. I tell her I love her and God has placed all her teachers in authority to act on His behalf just as He has given me that same authority as a parent. I tell her to remember who she is representing—Christ. And for her to be a good example to others. If Jesus is not in the school, it's because you didn't equip or arm your child/children with Him and the Word of God.

Also, my prayer in the morning is for God to place a hedge of protection around my daughter, the teachers, faculty members, and any other staff and volunteers. And lastly, I pray for a hedge of protection for all the children and the school.

In this fallen world, we never know what will happen from day to day. Make sure your children know how much you love them.

Be intentional. Be blessed.

# 223

Don't waste any more time. It's time to lock on to the things that you really love to do and pursue them with all of your heart. It's time to get serious about your relationship with God. Before you know it, you'll be standing in His presence, giving an account of what you did on earth. It's time to love the people you need to forgive. It's time to plug into your family. It's time to stop whining and to look for the good in your life. The matter is urgent. A blink of the eye, and you'll be gone.

Be intentional. Be blessed.

# 224

Do you know where your compass is?

The Bible is a moral compass to guide your life.

Struggling with pain, depression, anger, loneliness, or any other storms of life, open your Bible and take refuge because you are not alone.

If we are lost and not reading our compass, it cannot help us.

Be intentional. Be blessed.

# 225

Pray for *endurance* when you are faced with difficult situations and people.

"But I say to you, love your enemies, bless those who curse you, do good to those who hate you, and pray for those who spitefully use you and persecute you" (Matt. 5:44, NKJV).

I can testify that when you remain faithful and do what's right no matter the situation, God will bless you!

Be intentional. Be blessed.

# 226

Take time to pray for:
I am praying for singles
I am praying for our children
I am praying for single mothers
I am praying for single fathers
I am praying for the motherless
I am praying for the fatherless
I am praying for the widow
I am praying for the widower
I am praying for husbands and wives
I am praying for all
May you all be lifted up and encouraged.
Be intentional. Be blessed.

# 227

Taking our eyes off of self, we can then look to others and bless them.
What if we were more selfless and less selfish?
Be intentional. Be blessed.

# 228

When we give freely and do the work for God's kingdom, we change people's lives.

Be intentional. Be blessed.

# 229

Give me peace when I cannot improve circumstances and a prayerful heart for endurance toward that which I cannot change.

In the name of Jesus, I pray. Amen.

Be intentional. Be blessed.

# 230

If God benches you for a season, it's for a reason. Ask yourself, what is God trying to teach me?

Be intentional. Be blessed.

# 231

As I reflect back on years past, every year around this time, God has sent me on an incredible journey in my life into the unknown. I had had to face my childhood and other fears, all my past, and all my wounding along the way, but each year, there is something different that is very challenging and rewarding in my journey. I thank You, God, that You provide healing in Your name and You are making me new. As I embark on your newest journey for me today, I say thank You, Lord. Thank You for making the impossible possible.

Be intentional. Be blessed.

# 232

The mouth of a righteous man is a well of life,
but violence covereth the mouth of the wicked.

—Proverbs 10:11, KJV

Father, I pray for Your protection for those who are too weak to fight the evil that is inflicted on them through the violence of another. Help them to see your grace, love, and mercy, and to give them the strength to rise and prevail against the wicked. We know that we are not fighting flesh but against the powers, rulers of darkness, and spiritual wickedness. Father, wrap Your loving arms around them and provide a safe path to victory. We are more than conquerors through You! In Your precious name, I pray.

Amen.

Be intentional. Be blessed.

# 233

A lot of times, we are like whole trees planted firmly by the water. As years pass by being affected by pollution and toxic waste (lies, sins of other people, etc.), we start to get choked out slowly. Satan then slowly starts taking that ax to that tree because we have become weak and weary. Huge chunks are removed until there is all but a little left. Instead of being a whole tree, it is now reduced down to separate pieces and instead thrown into the fire for fuel; the fire devours both ends of it, its middle is burned. Is it now useful for any work? No. "When it was whole it could be but how much less will it be useful for any work when the fire has devoured it, and it is burned?" (Ezek. 15:4–5, MEV).

If we are not careful in guarding our gates by being faithful to God, reading the Word, praying, and worshipping God, then we could become just like the tree listed above. We are ultimately responsible for taking up our cross and getting healing in Jesus's name for our past, present, and current circumstances. We can't control the other person or circumstances, but we can control how we are affected by them. Remember we are also responsible and accountable before God for our own unfaithfulness to Him.

Be intentional. Be blessed.

# 234

They kept demanding an answer, so he stood up and said, "All right, but let the one who has never sinned throw the first stone!"

—John 8:7, NLT

We forget all too well that we *all* sin. Not just some of us, not just half of us, but *all* of us.

Think about this the next time you say, "I can't believe they did that." I too have been guilty of this, but I ask the Lord to help me to see them the way He sees them. It's never too late, and He will show you. Remember we are not exempt from that sin. The right set of circumstances and environment, and we could very well be in their shoes. Pray for them, bless them, and encourage them in the Lord. If you want to see someone's life impacted, show them Jesus!

Be intentional. Be blessed.

# 235

Reflecting back on this incredible journey from last year's conference to this one, I again come expectant! I am fully healed of trigeminal neuralgia. In Jesus's name, I boldly proclaim if He can do it for me, He can do it for you!

For all the miracles I have seen this year, God has used me as a humble vessel to bring His Holy healing from everything to cancer, to eardrum, to modern-day leprosy. You can do the same. Yes, *you*! He has called *you* to a time such as this! The same Spirit that raised Jesus from the dead resides and lives in you! He said in Luke 10:19 (NIV), "I have given you authority to trample on snakes and scorpions and to overcome all the power of the enemy; nothing will harm you."

Go bold. Go in Jesus's mighty name!

Be intentional. Be blessed.

# 236

As I reflect back on the years when I went through Elijah House, I can't help but be blown away by God's amazing work in my life so He can use me more effectively in His kingdom. All the sorrow and joy, tears and laughter, pain, and challenges of going through these classes resulted in the most rewarding experiences I have ever had in my life.

A huge thank you to my whole Elijah House family.

Facilitators, group leaders, small group leaders, mentors, and peers, I have learned so much from each one of you. Thank you for pouring into our lives so that we can be useful in God's kingdom.

Thank you, friends and family, who have supported me along my journey.

You all are truly a Blessing with a capital *B*!

"The law of the Lord is perfect, restoring the soul" (Ps. 19:7, NAS).

Be intentional. Be blessed.

# 237

Feelings of despair, I know it because I lived it. All those feelings: being scared, broken, dirty, used, worthless, unlovable, abandoned, lonely, abused physically and mentally, you name it. But I am living proof today of a Lord who *redeems*. If He can do it for me, He can do it for anyone else.

As a child, we don't get a choice, but as an adult, we do. We can choose to step into our God-given destiny or lay in our brokenness. I am so thankful for the godly people the Lord has placed in my path to mentor me; to help me get the healing I needed from these things; to encourage me; and even to model what godly, healthy, loving, family looks like and acts like. If I hadn't had a godly intervention, I would be a complete and total wreck as an adult. All it takes is an encounter with Jesus, and you will never be the same.

We may have had earthly broken parents who abused us, abandoned us, didn't love us, and left us. But our Heavenly Father thinks we are amazing! We are to die for, and He fulfilled all of this by dying on a cross so that we could be redeemed. It's time to take off the brokenness shame, etc., and take up our cross and follow Him! Mentor the broken, children and adults alike. Show them the way, the truth, and the life—Jesus.

I still remember the day I was taken from my mother and placed into foster care. It serves as a memorial for the day the hardest, but most rewarding part of my life began. Could I see it then as a broken child? No way. Can I see it absolutely now? See, you never know what someone has been through or is walking through. It may be the battle of their life. And if you do know what they are walking into or through, make sure you are building them up instead of tearing them down because one day, you will have to give an account for these things, things you did here on earth. And I know when I get to Heaven, I want to hear the words of my Heavenly Father, my "Daddy" say, "Well done, my loyal and faithful servant."

I want to leave a godly legacy full of fruit—fruit of the spirit, of godly character—not only for my generation but the future generations coming behind me.

Be intentional. Be blessed.

# 238

Happy Mother's Day today and every day. My beautiful gift from God surprises me more and more each day. Her smiles, her contagious laughter, how her eyes twinkle in the light, her perspective, reminding me to literally stop and smell the roses. The entrustment the Lord has given me with her is such an honor.

To my mother Marie, I honor you today. If there had been no you, I wouldn't have been here. Thank you for deciding not to abort me when you had cancer, and the doctors were insisting that you do. That little 4-pound miracle that had a rough start at life is beating the odds thanks to you and God. I empathize and honor you for who you are in Christ. What you have been through in this lifetime, no person should have ever have had to go through, but it helps me to understand now as a grown adult why I am so thankful I have been a part of your journey, praying together, loving you, showing you the love Christ. Though hundreds of miles away, I love you and miss you dearly.

To my spiritual mamas and mentors, I honor you and thank you for your love and guidance, equipping, encouraging, and helping me to grow in Christ. Thank you for being true examples of godly women. Your impact on my life will forever be cherished.

To my friends and family who are mothers, I honor you today as well. To whom much is given, much is required. Remember every day is a gift and how we choose to unwrap it can impact our children and the generations coming behind us. Make sure you be the change you want to see.

For we know that we can do *all* things through Christ who strengthens us.

"For the ones who have lost their children, can't have children, or any who have other circumstances; whatever it is, I honor you and have already prayed for you this morning" (Phil. 4:13).

The Lord is near to the brokenhearted.

Be intentional. Be blessed.

# 239

Therefore, since we are surrounded by such a huge crowd of witnesses to the life of faith, let us strip off every weight that slows us down, especially the sin that so easily trips us up. And let us run with endurance the race God has set before us.

—Hebrews 12:1, NLT

We really are surrounded by such a great cloud of witnesses to the life of faith, and how we live out this life that is before us can impact someone else's life. There is always someone watching, waiting, expecting you to be who you say you are. That doesn't mean you have a perfect life, but it means you pursue righteousness. Right standing with the Lord at all cost because at the end of this life, we will all have to give an account of ourselves before the Lord of the who, what, where, when, why, and the how. Take notice: I didn't say give an account of what your friends, children, girlfriend, boyfriend, or your spouse did. They have their own personal relationship with the Lord that they should be pursuing, if they are young children, yes, it is your job to guide them until they can sustain themselves.

"Train up a child in the way he should go: and when he is old, he will not depart from it" (Prov. 22:6, KJV).

Time for inspection. If you are going through a storm in life, ask some of these questions for a starting point.

1. How am I responding to these circumstances?

Though painful, am I counting it all joy as I am walking through these trials of life because my God is bigger than my current circumstances? Or am I blasting it all over Facebook talking about it more than I have prayed about it? This does not mean you can't post anything about what you are walking through and get prayer and counsel. In fact, I encourage anyone who is going through something to seek wise biblical counsel. Get an awesome godly mentor. Surround yourself with godly people who tell you when you are off-track but help you to get back on. It's okay not to be okay; we just can't stay there permanently. Be open to correction and training so that you can participate in true Christian discipleship. It is God's will for our lives to be healed and be made whole.

2. What does my fruit look like?

Am I already in season and out of season?

Do I look bitter and beaten down? Do I look like what I am walking through? Or do I have the reflection of Christ, the joy of the Lord, so much so that it encourages someone else who is walking through something to seek out God with all of their heart. After all, if God could do it for me, He surely will do it for you! We should have Christ's countenance. We should radiate His reflection to include His character.

And if I am not, what steps do I need to take to get there?

3. Do I have the mind of Christ? Am I renewing my mind?

"Don't copy the behavior and customs of this world, but let God transform you into a new person by changing the way you think. Then you will learn to know God's will for you, which is good and pleasing and perfect" (Rom. 12:2, NLT).

Dig into His Word, your Bible. Know when the evil one is battling you in your mind, will, and emotions. Know how to rebuke him in the mighty name of Jesus!

If you don't know how to rebuke the evil one, ask someone you trust that does know. I have heard it said many times: What would I go to a biblical counselor for? So that they can tell me how messed up I am?

No, that's your job to tell them so that they can help you develop a plan for Godliness, healthiness, wholeness, and live it out. They can help you only as far as you are willing and honest to reveal.

We worry too much about others, and the evil one likes to play the shame game. *What if I see someone I know in the counseling office or they see me asking for help?*

Well, let's see: Realize that the evil one is trying to shame you and keep you in bondage. Change the stinking thinking, and be encouraged that they have stuff too. You are not the only one, and they are seeking wholeness and healing right along with you so you can be happy for your brother or sister in Christ instead of being miserable. It's actually freeing, and where the Lord is, there is freedom. After all, it's not like you have some neon sign above your head that says what your problems are, but the truth is, that's the way we act. You don't have to stay in isolation, and isolation or freedom is a choice. God never meant for us to, so every day, you and I can choose. Are we closer to bondage or freedom?

What will it be?

Be intentional. Be blessed.

# 240

Why do you want to be somebody else when you could be ten times better if you could just find it in yourself? That's right; you have already been given everything that pertains to life and Godliness. The Holy Spirit resides within you. So instead of wishing you were someone else, just be be-*you*-ti-ful or just be handsome!

He said you are fearfully and wonderfully made, so embrace it knowing as you ought to know and boldly proclaiming, "I am a daughter or son of the Highest. I have been bought with a price. I am to die for." This is not obtainable in worldly confidence but can only be found in godly confidence. Knowing who you are in Christ and the Holy Spirit who resides in you can change everything! When your identity is stable in Christ, you won't look to things or people to define you. You won't need to play the comparison game because you will know your real value and worth, and that comes only from knowing and having an authentic, intimate relationship with Him.

"Those who are wise will shine like the brightness of the heavens, and those who lead many to righteousness, like the stars for ever and ever" (Dan. 12:3, NIV).

Be intentional. Be blessed.

# 241

I pray this book of memoirs has been an encouragement and blessing to you as the reader. May we never forget that our true identity is found in the intimate relationship between us and our Heavenly Father. You have been set apart and called to a time such as this.

> May the Lord: Bless you and keep you
> The Lord make His face shine upon you
> And be gracious to you
> The Lord lift up His countenance upon you,
> And give you peace (Num. 6:24–26, NKJV)

"Write His name on you and say you belong to me," said Pastor Rusty Nelson.
Amen.

# Acknowledgments

To all my friends and family who have walked this journey with me, who have laughed, cried, and encouraged me through the toughest of times.

To all my spiritual mamas, pastors, counselors, and leaders, I am forever grateful for you pouring into my life and helping me to restore my identity and find my eternal worth in God.

A special thank you to Pam and Lana for the sister celebration in honor of God and the celebration of *Memoirs of Elohim and I.*

To my sisters, Wilma, Sheila, Romana-Gail, and my brother Anthony, I love you all dearly. To my nieces Lexi, Allie, Macy, and Star, and to my nephews Christopher, Daniel, Trevor, John, William, Chance, and William-Grayson each one of you is so special to me, and God has a specific plan and a purpose for your life.

# About the Author

Cristy Castleberry is a single mom of one beautiful girl. She is a prayer warrior who finds delight in the most secret and most intimate places with her Heavenly Father. She is an advocate for seeing God restore identity while turning victims into victors, the conquered into conquerors, the wounded into the wanted, the rejected into the redeemed, the harmed into the healed, and the real messes of our lives turned into messages. Her most significant privilege is to do the work for God's kingdom. Her passion for God's kingdom compels her to serve at church, in her community, and to lead a life group in her home.

CPSIA information can be obtained
at www.ICGtesting.com
Printed in the USA
LVHW091011181118
597554LV00001B/31/P